2.21.06

~
To Marvin _

One of
the original Reagan
loyalists. ~Thanks
for your support.
May all your
communications
be "The Greatest."

All the best,

The Greatest
Communicator

The Greatest Communicator

What Ronald Reagan Taught Me about Politics, Leadership, and Life

DICK WIRTHLIN

WITH

WYNTON C. HALL

John Wiley & Sons, Inc.

Illustration credits: Page 82 (top), photo by Dennis Brack/Black Star. All other photos courtesy of the Ronald Reagan Library.

Published by John Wiley & Sons, Inc., Hoboken, New Jersey
Published simultaneously in Canada

Design and production by Navta Associates, Inc.

For general information about our other products and services, please contact our Customer Care Department within the United States at (800) 762-2974, outside the United States at (317) 572-3993 or fax (317) 572-4002.

Wiley also publishes its books in a variety of electronic formats. Some content that appears in print may not be available in electronic books. For more information about Wiley products, visit our web site at www.wiley.com.

Library of Congress Cataloging-in-Publication Data

Wirthlin, Richard.
   The greatest communicator : what Ronald Reagan taught me about politics, leadership, and life / Richard B. Wirthlin with Wynton C. Hall.
      p. cm.
   ISBN 0-471-70509-8 (cloth : alk. paper)
   1. Reagan, Ronald—Friends and associates. 2. Wirthlin, Richard. 3. Political consultants—United States—Biography. 4. Reagan, Ronald—Political and social views. 5. Reagan, Ronald. 6. Presidents—United States—Biography. 7. Friendship—United States—Case studies. 8. Political campaigns—United States—History—20th century. 9. United States—Politics and government—1945–1989. I. Hall, Wynton C., 1976– II. Title.
   E877.2.W57 2005
   973.927'092—dc22   2004015427

To my father, Joseph L. Wirthlin,
and mother, Madeline Bitner Wirthlin,
who taught the values of both compassionate
public service and principled politics

Contents

Photographs follow page 81

Preface

This is not a book about what I did for Ronald Reagan, but about what he did for the world. From 1968 to 1988 I was privileged to serve as his pollster and chief strategist. In that time, as a former professor of economics, I became a student again. Indeed, those of us who were at Reagan's side from the beginning will tell you that he gave us more than we ever imagined. We will tell you that our lives are forever better for having worked in his shadow. And we will mean it.

Still, no president's rise to power comes easily. Leadership is always a battle waged at incalculable costs—both personal and professional. Tension and tragedy are often preludes to triumph, and we experienced them all: bitter campaign defeats, high-stakes presidential debates, tense meetings in the Oval Office, the "Evil Empire," Reykjavik, "Tear down this wall," the assassination attempt, the Geneva summit, reelection in 1984, a graceful exit in the face of Alzheimer's. These memories ricochet through my mind and remind me of how blessed America was to have been led by a man some have called "the last lion of the twentieth century."

Historians, commentators, and scholars have tried to pinpoint the mystery of Reagan's greatness. And sadly, even as Nancy struggled during his last years to shower her husband with patience and dignity, a good many more did their level best to raze the president's legacy. As painful as this was to witness, something tells me that had he been able, Reagan would cock his head to the side with that trademark twinkle in his eye and grin. The Irishman in him always loved a good fight, especially when the stakes were high. But more than that, Ronald Reagan believed absorbing blows from critics was simply the price a man must pay in order to follow his life's calling. Reagan's calling: comforting and protecting people to build a strong and secure base for America's future. And any man who finds himself on the receiving end of an assassin's bullet fully understands the costs leadership exacts. Leaders who never face fierce opposition are not leaders at all. Reagan knew this.

And he knew other things, as well.

He believed that liberty is the essence of man; evil is strong; God is stronger; and that many of America's greatest heroes are often among her least celebrated. These beliefs were consciously embedded in the words Ronald Reagan spoke, and they mirrored his belief that America remains "the last best hope for mankind." Such a view is, of course, fitting. For it reflects not only the nature of America, but also the nature of the man I was privileged to serve. A man I will always consider the Greatest Communicator.

Acknowledgments

My life was blessed because of Ronald Reagan and those whom I met and worked with because of him.

To communicate with conviction, passion, and power was one of Ronald Reagan's great gifts. But even more important was the impact his words had on the nation and the world. He changed both for the better during the 1980s—the Reagan decade. The nuclear cloud of Mutually Assured Destruction that hung heavily over the entire earth was lifted. The twin economic demons of rampant inflation and high unemployment were caged. And Reagan accomplished both of these goals because he was freedom's most effective spokesman.

There are many who assisted in launching and sustaining the Reagan Revolution, but none were more important than Nancy Reagan. She was Ronald Reagan's ultimate confidante and most committed defender. Without her, there might never have been the Revolution at all.

Because of Ronald Reagan, I met and learned from the original Reaganauts and from those actively involved in his campaigns and his administration. They were, among others, Ed Meese, Lyn Nofziger, Marty Anderson, Dick Richards, Peter Hannaford, Mike Deaver, Paul Laxalt, Bill Clark, Holmes Tuttle, Alan Greenspan, George Schultz, Richard Allen, Jim Baker, Don Regan, Howard Baker, Ken Duberstein,

David Gergen, Tony Dolan, and, finally, Bill Casey, who not only brought much-needed order and focus to the 1980 campaign, but served the president well as the director of the CIA.

The political components of Ronald Reagan's first run for the governorship of California were crafted before I met him with help from Stu Spencer, Bill Roberts, Vince Barabba, Patty Mordigan, and others.

In the two races for the presidency, I was privileged to work with some of the most talented and effective advertising executives in the country—Peter Dailey, Phil Dusenberry, Hal Riney. They magnified Reagan's political reach by knowing early that television and radio were most powerful when they allowed Reagan to be Reagan.

Thanks also go to Roger Ailes, Bay Buchanan, James Carville, Karl Rove, Peter Hart, Fred Barnes, Chris Wallace, and the Ronald Reagan Library for helping me retrace the footprints of the Revolution.

Without the expertise of the members of my planning and strategy group—John Moss, Vince Breglio, John Fiedler, Richard Beal, with the assistance of Gary Lawrence, Ron Hinckley, and Charles Rund—whatever contribution I made to the 1976, 1980, and 1984 campaigns would have been severely diminished. Further, Tom Reynolds's fertile and creative mind provided key strategic insights over the Reagan years.

I am grateful for the present leadership of WirthlinWorldwide—Dee Allsop, Dave Richardson, Joel White, Jim Hoskins—for the gracious support they have given this project, and to my assistants who have helped me in so many ways over the years: Kathy Klotz, Celeste Heritage, and Geri Bartholomew. To Linda Johnson, who, because of her White House training, can find almost anyone, anywhere, anytime for me, I express sincere gratitude.

I extend my thanks to John Wiley & Sons, including publisher Kitt Allan, senior marketing manager Laura Cusack, freelance copy editor Roland Ottewell, and senior production editor Hope Breeman. Special thanks go to our editor, Hana Lane, whose skill and commitment ensured this project's timely completion. Her guidance was sage and her support indefatigable.

Without the skill of our agent, Joe Vallely, who opened the doors at Wiley so rapidly, this book might have become just one of a myriad of afterthoughts about Ronald Reagan.

Grateful thanks also go to Peter and Rochelle Schweizer, Patrick Smith, Jenna Miley, Marty Medhurst, Katie Hall, and Bainbridge College for their continued support throughout the writing of this book.

In addition to the above-mentioned, credit deserves to be shared with all those who marched cheerfully in the Reagan Revolution, and all those who walked precincts, knocked on doors, and offered support on Reagan's behalf. Chief among the president's supporters was President George H. W. Bush, whose loyalty and leadership remain an example to all Americans.

I express my enduring appreciation to Wynton Hall, friend and academic colleague, who carefully reviewed hundreds of thousands of my documents concerning the Reagan presidency and patiently listened to my reflections about why Ronald Reagan was the Greatest Communicator. He brought all those disparate sources together that made this book possible.

I also wish to express love and appreciation for my children and grandchildren, the true benefactors of the Reagan legacy, who bring me joy unimaginable.

And most importantly, I recognize with great gratitude the support of my wife, Jeralie, who was always there for me in times of both shadow and sunshine.

The author alone is responsible for the contents of this book.

Prologue

Great" versus "Greatest"
Communicators

I wasn't a great communicator.
—Ronald Reagan, Farewell Address, January 11, 1989

On February 23, 1984, I walked into the Oval Office and found the president standing beside his desk holding what appeared to be a photograph.

"Mr. President, what's that you've got there?" I asked.

"Well, Dick, I just got off the phone with this young man." As the president turned the photograph around for me to view, I winced at the haunting image staring me in the face. It was the picture of a twelve-year-old boy who had been severely burned while attempting to rescue his two younger brothers when their family's trailer caught fire. The first brother he found easily, and simply passed through the window. Saving the second brother, however, proved much more difficult. While frantically searching through the flaming trailer, the young man sustained severe burns before carrying his sibling to safety. As a result, the president explained, the boy's face and body had been seriously scarred and disfigured.

"I called this little fella to see how he was doing and to tell him how proud I was of his heroism," Reagan said.

Still shaken by the image, I struggled to get something out. "I'm sure he appreciated your call, Mr. President."

As he looked back down at the little boy's visage, a smile spread slowly across the president's face. "Dick, at the end of our conversation the youngster said, 'President Reagan, I sure wish I would have had my tape recorder on so I could remember our call together.' So I said, 'Do you have it there?' He said he did. So I told him, 'Well, son, turn it on and let's chat some more.'"

Did you catch that?

"Let's chat some more?" The busiest and most powerful man on the planet saying to a little boy, "Let's chat some more"?

This is the language of leadership. These aren't the words of a great communicator. These are the words of one of the *greatest* communicators. There is, I have found, a difference.

Merely "great" communicators stir the collective passions of audiences. Amid the din of cheers, great communicators touch both hearts and minds. They gesture strategically, pause purposefully, and enunciate clearly. As the audience sends forth a tidal wave of applause, great communicators exit the stage and, like Clark Kent entering his phone booth in reverse, transform themselves into lesser versions of their former oratorical selves. We have all experienced this before. A speaker, perhaps a CEO or a community leader, delivers a dynamic speech. But then, when you meet them one-on-one, they begin to shrink before your very eyes. Their cadence shifts, their passion subsides, and as a result their motives seem less certain than when the power of the podium was working in their favor. Great onstage, lackluster off.

The greatest communicators are different.

These are people for whom the curtain's presence or absence makes little difference—they are the same person behind it as they are in front. They communicate consistently. There is no noticeable beginning to their public persona or end to their private self. They are, in a sense, seamless. When people say that Ronald Reagan was "the Great Communicator," they are only correct by half. Reagan was among the greatest of communicators because he mastered not only public communication but interpersonal communication as well.

After having worked at Ronald Reagan's side for over two decades, one of my greatest regrets is that most Americans saw only glimpses of their president's ability to communicate interpersonally. For those on the outside, it was easy to dismiss Reagan as just an "actor," as a person playing the role of president. But a man cannot feign humanity.

Moments like the one the president shared on the phone with that little boy were the moments Reagan cherished most. Sure, stories like those won't be remembered a hundred years from now or fill the textbooks schoolchildren read, but they still matter. They matter to the hundreds of people who have handwritten letters penned by the president hanging on the walls of their homes, preserved in simple frames. They are important to the people who tell stories at family reunions about the time they got a phone call or a letter from the president of the United States. Not one of those form letters signed by a machine that replicates a president's scrawl—a real letter, written only the way Ronald Reagan could.

Trust me. They matter.

Some presidents love policy. Ronald Reagan loved people. It was, after all, his passion for the latter that prompted his interest in the former. And he would seek opportunities to communicate with those in need. Looking back, even before I knew him, he was always this way. Like many children born to an alcoholic parent, he was heir to the bittersweet gift of a consoling and protective spirit. So it was only natural he would gravitate toward jobs where he could protect people or bring them happiness. Whether literally saving lives (seventy-seven lives, to be exact) as a lifeguard in the cool waters of Rock River in Illinois, delivering lines of inspiration in *Knute Rockne—All-American* and *King's Row*, or indulging listeners in the great American escape from reality as a radio sports announcer for WHO in Des Moines, Reagan was the consummate consoler.

And now this man who knew how to touch people with his words and deeds had a bigger vehicle through which to inspire—national public service. Regardless of whether we were on Air Force One, in the Oval Office, or in a less than glamorous hotel out on the campaign trail, Ronald Reagan always made it clear to me how important words were to him. Whether face-to-face, on television, in handwritten missives, or through radio, Reagan's communications conveyed a sense of intimacy and warmth, regardless of venue. Why did he take his ability to communicate so seriously? Simply put, because he saw it as an opportunity to build relationships.

This book is about the relationship I witnessed Ronald Reagan forge with the American people through his greatest gift: the ability to change lives—indeed, the world—with words. Luckily, over the span of a four-decade friendship, I heeded the advice my mother gave me as a young boy. "Remember," she would say, "the palest ink outlasts the strongest memory." Her respect for history—and sense of duty that it be preserved—stayed with me throughout my life.

And so, through the years I kept contemporaneous memos for the record, a diary, and a storage house packed with private memoranda, opinion research studies, and strategy documents produced on Ronald Reagan's behalf. Publishers came knocking, but the time never felt quite right. Until one day, after discussing my remembrances with a friend, I realized that so many stories and memories had taken place when there was no one else in the room but Reagan and me. This book is my attempt to preserve those moments and to pay tribute to the man I served and the friend I'll never forget.

Of course, the many stories I will share in the pages that follow had already begun to vanish nearly a decade before the president's passing. He couldn't remember the time he almost gave me an ulcer when he asked me to buy an anniversary card for him to give to Nancy from the sparse selection at Dulles Airport; or the scores of times we sat in the Oval Office cracking jokes while combing through my polling data; or the time he had Secret Service agents pull me right out of the center of the reception line at my son's wedding in Los Angeles so they could put me on a secure phone where, at the president's suggestion, I was informed he was going to begin bombing Libya and wanted my advice; or even when he and Nancy would sit in their pajamas in the White House residence where I would occasionally go over strategy with them. These are just some of the many snapshots, the mental mementos I carried in my heart and mind, even as they had vanished from his.

In the sunset of his life, Alzheimer's grip suffocated the vitality that once marked my friend's spirit. There was to be no more riding of horses, telling of jokes, delivering of speeches, or writing of love letters to his "darling Nancy." The fortieth president of the United States had no recollection of being one of the greatest communicators the world has ever known, or that for eight years he was its most powerful inhabitant. Like a master painter who's lost his ability to see colors, most cruel of all, the president had been robbed of his ability to speak. But perhaps there is a tragic beauty in this, Ronald Reagan's final communicative lesson whispered to us all: *Our words are our legacy, an inheritance we leave to those who can use what we no longer can.*

Short.

Simple.

Profound.

Just the way the Greatest Communicator would have wanted it.

1

The Beginning of a Beautiful Friendship

Meeting Ronald Reagan, 1968

Louis, I think this is the beginning of a beautiful friendship.

—the line Ronald Reagan was to deliver as "Rick,"
Humphrey Bogart's character, in the movie *Casablanca*

Just one month following Ronald Reagan's 1984 landslide reelection victory, the president and I met in the Oval Office. He looked well rested that day, and I remember feeling like he hadn't aged a bit over the last four years. As Reagan got up from his desk to sit in his usual seat in front of the fireplace, he stopped at the window.

"Dick, how do you like my friend over there?" he asked.

I couldn't see what he was pointing to, so I walked to the window looking out over the Rose Garden. Curled up on one of the seats outside was a white and gray tabby cat.

"He's been there for the last two or three days," Reagan said. "I think he's made that chair his home."

"Mr. President," I replied, "I'd say that's pretty elegant and exclusive surroundings for a plain old alley cat."

Reagan just smiled and chuckled before sitting down by the fireplace.

When I think about the way Ronald Reagan viewed himself, I sometimes think of that little alley cat. Like his four-legged White House visitor, Reagan believed he had wandered into the greatest honor on earth. The way he saw it, he was just an ordinary man who had been given an extraordinary opportunity. I, on the other hand, never saw it quite that way. To me, Reagan's talent and vision were anything but "ordinary." He was the most gifted leader I've ever known. But he never thought in those terms. Giving credit to others was always his way. I can still picture the little bronzed placard that sat on his desk: "There is no limit to what you can accomplish if you don't care who gets the credit." His lack of pretense and humble spirit were two of the things that drew me to him the first time we met, in 1968.

All of us who worked closely with Ronald Reagan have a story to tell about the first time we met him, but mine is a little different. It came about in the fall of 1968 when then governor Reagan wanted to hire me anonymously to conduct an opinion survey for him.

I learned two essential truths about Ronald Reagan during our first encounter on a sun-drenched day in California. First, Reagan was no "amiable dunce," as Clark Clifford once infamously called him. And second, this was a man who understood how to use words to win hearts and minds.

At the time, I was a visiting professor of economics at Arizona State University. Four years earlier at Brigham Young University, I had started doing some polling and consulting on the side. Back then my politics were somewhat mixed. When I was a boy growing up in Utah, my mother was chairperson of the Women's Republican Club of Utah. So I had always considered myself a Republican. When I was a PhD student at the University of California at Berkeley, my friends thought I was an "ultra-conservative," but when I was a professor at BYU my politics were thought moderate by most and even liberal by a few.

The academic life was filled with intellectual energy and excitement. But by 1968, other opportunities had begun to emerge. And this opportunity changed my life forever.

It all started with a phone call. The person on the other end introduced himself as one "Tom Green" from New York. Mr. Green said he wanted to hire me to conduct a public opinion survey of Californians' attitudes about a host of policy issues, as well as voters' impressions of various state leaders. Naturally, I wanted to know more—who would use the numbers and how would the data be applied? But the client remained cryptic. All he would say was that more information would be forthcoming once the polling was complete. To allay any concerns I might have about his ability to fund the study, Green gave me some references to verify his financial means. Today, when I think about it, I sometimes wonder why the secretive nature of it all didn't raise any red flags. But, for whatever reason, it didn't.

I put the finishing touches on the final report a few weeks later. Green and I agreed I would fly to Los Angeles for a face-to-face meeting where I would present my data to my mysterious client. We met at the International Hotel on Century Boulevard near the Los Angeles Airport. As soon as the words "Hello, Mr. Green" crossed my lips, the man interrupted me. "Actually, my name isn't really Mr. Green. It's Tom Reed" (a well-known California political operative). Thoroughly confused, I asked where the meeting would be held, but he wouldn't budge. An evasive "You'll see" was as far as he was willing to go. So Reed and I hopped into a limousine and cruised toward the California hills. As we hit the San Diego Freeway heading north, he explained that I would be discussing my information with a party of one, the governor of the state, Ronald Reagan.

I don't think I'll ever forget that ride. My traveling companion remained silent. The freeway was clogged, making the drive seem even longer than it was. Worse, the roads nearing the Reagan home were riddled with curves. Whoever built those roads must have been in love with hairpin turns, because it felt like we were driving in a never-ending spiral, which only added to my anxiety. Meanwhile, Reed would not tell me how my data would be used. I tried not to fidget. This whole scenario—complete with fictitious names, tortuous roads, and a stoic limo driver—was starting to feel more and more like a scene out of *The Godfather* than a legitimate business enterprise. But finally we arrived at a beautiful, ranch-style home that sparkled in the California sun.

You know those rare moments when you just know *something major, something life-changing, is about to happen? Well, for me, this was one of those moments.*

The car came to a halt and a casually dressed and smiling Governor Ronald Reagan emerged from his front door. I made a mental note about how much it impressed me that the governor of the most populous state in the union would welcome us as we made our way up the driveway.

"Hi, Dick. Ronald Reagan. So nice to meet you. Please, come in."

Little did I know that the hand clasping mine belonged to the man who would become one of my dearest, lifelong friends. And if someone had told me that the actor-turned-governor standing before me would lead America brilliantly for eight years as president, win the cold war, and change the contours of human history, I might not have believed them. You see, at that point in time I had bought into many of the myths about Reagan. Frankly, I thought he was politically to the right of Attila the Hun! I had unthinkingly swallowed many of the cynical lines created by the governor's opponents: "he's a political lightweight," "an extremist who recites right-wing dogma," "a simpleton whose biggest accomplishment is that his name has scrolled the screens of Hollywood's B-movie list." In sum, the rap on Reagan was that he could not lead; that rather, he was easily led. Characterizations such as these revealed the great chasm between fact and fiction operative in the minds of Reagan's opponents and, for a time, in mine as well.

"Thanks so much, Dick, for making the trip out to the house."

"Governor, it's a pleasure to be here with you. I didn't know we were going to meet today," I confessed, "but it's an honor nonetheless."

Now, you've got to appreciate this scene: Here I am, a Mormon professor of economics—a statistician—dressed in a brown polyester suit, standing across from the actor who was originally cast to play the role of Rick (Humphrey Bogart's debonair character) in the cinematic classic *Casablanca*. As if the contrast between us wasn't stark enough, Reagan was wearing a pair of expertly tailored white slacks and a stylish checkered shirt with the top two buttons left casually undone so as to expose a golden tan reminiscent of the Hollywood Hills at sunset. A farm boy from a small smelter town in Utah turned academic meeting with a bona fide Hollywood movie star turned governor?

I felt about as comfortable as a fish swimming in a bowl of wet cement.

Tom Reed said goodbye before hopping back into the limo, leaving me alone with the governor. Reagan invited me inside his home, and it was there that I first met Nancy. After greeting me warmly, she asked what we would like to drink. "Dick and I will have two fruit juices, please," Reagan said. We made our way into his library overlooking the family swimming pool. Nancy brought us our drinks, and as she did, the governor broke the ice with his trademark wit.

"So, Dick, did you enjoy yourself at Berkeley? Nancy thinks it's terrible there. She doesn't believe in free love."

"Oh, Ronnie. Stop that." Nancy giggled.

Grinning, I said, "Well, honestly, I pre-dated all that, Governor. In 1964 I took a job at Brigham Young, where I chaired the economics department and reestablished and directed the survey research center."

Sitting across from Reagan, I guess the first thing that struck me most in those initial fifteen minutes or so was his interest in me as a person, not as a pollster. We talked about family and church and our mutual interest in policies designed to help those living in poverty. He wasn't just interested in "getting down to business," like so many politicians I've worked with. To him, getting to know someone *was* his business. He asked questions and listened. Indeed, many years later, Reagan once told an audience, "When Dick Wirthlin speaks, I listen!" But the truth is Reagan believed *everyone* deserved an attentive ear.

For example, the former prime minister of Canada, Brian Mulroney, tells a story about the time he overheard former French president François Mitterrand say of Ronald Reagan that he "is not so much a Great Communicator—although he is—as someone in *communion* with the American people." On that point, Mitterrand was absolutely correct.

As we talked, Reagan skillfully directed the conversation to the many things he and I had in common. We had both studied economics in college and grown up in middle American farm communities defined by faith and family. What's more, he was an incurable optimist, as am I. Topic after topic, at every turn, he built communicative bridges with ease.

After chatting for a while, it was finally time to discuss my survey data. I can honestly say that Ronald Reagan proved to be one of the most empirically astute clients I've ever had. Throughout my career as a strategist, I've always used a little test to determine a client's level of intellectual curiosity. Before explaining my findings, I take ten minutes to explain the statistical design of a client's survey. Often, the individual will nod approvingly, in a hurried way, as if to say nonverbally, "Yeah,

yeah, yeah. Enough with the statistical mumbo-jumbo. What's the bottom line? What do you recommend I say?"

But that's not how Reagan responded. He interrupted me with questions about my sample, about the margin of error, about the way a question was worded. And he did it in a way that showed he understood the strengths and weaknesses of survey research. After all, Reagan was no stranger to numbers. He had majored in economics at Eureka College, so he understood that data is only as valuable as the method used to collect it. Moreover, he wasn't interested in being told *what* to say—he intrinsically knew that. He was interested in the most effective way to convey his message. But most importantly, he never lost sight of what all those numbers I shuffled in front of him were really all about.

Many years later during a speech commemorating my firm's twenty-fifth anniversary, Ronald Reagan explained the thoughts that had filled his mind every time we sat down and sifted through the myriad pages of my polling data: "For every number, I saw a face. The numbers represented the people, and we had to remember that the people are the ones who sent us there." I'm glad he said those words aloud. But the simple truth is, he didn't need to. I knew as much the very first day I met him.

Like the photograph of the little boy with whom he had spoken on the phone, for Reagan, a person's countenance was a map. In the midst of a president's frenetic daily pace, I suppose the human face represented a shorthand way to remain grounded and mindful of those he was charged to lead. If you think about it, it makes perfect sense. Speakers spend the bulk of their lives staring out at an ocean of faces. When a president is leading a country of over 200 million people, the face connects him to the reality of that endeavor and reminds him of the lives his leadership affects.

Interestingly, the voters I had polled on Reagan's behalf in that very first study felt the same way about the power of the human face and its capacity to communicate. Among the reams of numbers dealing with questions about education, taxes, and campus riots had been a crop of queries on voters' views of various California political figures. When they were asked for their impressions of the governor, one of Reagan's most frequently cited strengths was his ability to speak. Even among people who were intent on voting for another candidate or who were undecided, Reagan rated highly. One number in particular sprung off the page: 64 percent of those interviewed said they were impressed with Reagan's ability to communicate through television. Voters enjoyed seeing his face and listening to him speak. I decided to tuck this finding away in my mental filing cabinet for later use.

But that day, sitting in the library of his Pacific Palisades home, I watched Reagan operate one-on-one in close quarters, unobstructed by the glare of a television screen. When he gave voice to his vision and values, the façade of fame and the pretense of power were erased from my mind. My preconceptions of a heavy-handed, right-wing Hollywood actor had been wrong from the start. Like the millions of voters who would later elect him president, I found that Reagan's belief in America's promise and his innate optimism paralleled my own. Better still, there was nothing Machiavellian about him. He just had a way of making me feel like we were connected to something much larger than ourselves. He had more raw leadership ability than anyone I had ever seen. And whether I realized it then or not, the synergy of his words, values, and vision would forever change the way I viewed political strategy and leadership.

When we were finished with our meeting, Nancy and the governor walked me to the door. Just as quickly as they had vanished, Tom Reed and the limo driver had reappeared and were waiting outside. I turned to face Reagan and shook his hand before getting in the car. As we pulled out of the driveway, I glanced back at the two of them waving from their doorstep.

Speeding through the California hills, I thought about how different the Reagan I had just met was from the caricature constructed by his critics. They tried to paint him in bellicose hues, as a man of unbending and strident spirit. But he wasn't. He was a gentle man with a desire for helping others.

Yet for all his gentleness, Reagan relished a good fight. I mean he actually *enjoyed* it. I picked up on this that day as well. During our discussions he had mentioned he wanted me to conduct future studies. Having now met him face-to-face, I was eager to do so. Since he had already dipped his toes into the presidential pool with a short-lived run in the 1968 Republican presidential primary, it didn't seem entirely implausible to assume he might have his eyes on the White House. Given California's large number of electoral votes, governors of the state are frequently on the short list of presidential contenders. Still, that fact aside, I sensed Reagan was a fighter in search of a larger battle. Not out of vanity or a desire for raw power, but out of a sense that his life's calling would require him to expand his sphere of influence in order to touch more lives.

Settling in back home, I had just one last nagging question: Why had Ronald Reagan's operative, Tom Reed (aka "Mr. Green"), called *me* to conduct his study? The answer would come from an unlikely source, a former client of mine, Barry Goldwater.

One thing I've learned in all my years in politics is that there are people who, under the cover of darkness and without your knowledge, may have worked tirelessly to hurt your relationship with a candidate. For example, on his deathbed, hardball Republican strategist Lee Atwater called me from the hospital to apologize for all the things he had done to cause me problems during the 1984 presidential election. What had Lee done to me? I wish I knew. To this day I haven't the slightest clue what "problems" he was referring to.

But I have found the reverse to be equally true. Like a

guardian angel operating in secret, sometimes your greatest ally is a person who does you a favor without your knowledge. Conservative icon Barry Goldwater was, for me, one such person.

A longtime admirer of Goldwater, Reagan had served as the co-chairman of the Arizona senator's 1964 presidential campaign in California. In that role, Reagan had rocketed to the top of the Republican Party's list of favorites when he delivered a televised speech on Goldwater's behalf now referred to simply as "The Speech." It was a rhetorical tour de force, a speech Reagan would later call one of the most important milestones of his political life. When Goldwater's conservative classic *The Conscience of a Conservative* was published, Reagan nodded along as he read. The two men shared an ideological symmetry on many issues. As a result, Barry's counsel carried significant weight with Reagan.

Goldwater later told me he and the Reagans had been discussing campaigning at a dinner party hosted by Nancy's father. Reagan was asked how he liked politics. He responded that it was an enjoyable challenge, but that he had learned it was difficult to find people he could really trust. That's when Goldwater gave me the endorsement of a lifetime. He said, "Ron, there are few people in politics you can trust absolutely, but Dick Wirthlin is one of those persons." That was all Reagan needed to hear.

It wouldn't be long before Reagan and I would watch his political star begin to shimmer. Yet the road to the White House is littered with the bruised hopes and broken dreams of many candidates. Before I could have my turn as his chief strategist, and before Reagan could become president, we would have to experience one of the most gut-wrenching losses in modern presidential campaign history. Ironically, Reagan's 1976 Republican primary defeat to Gerald Ford would sow the seeds of future presidential victory. Indeed, to this day I strongly believe that without that painful experience it is highly unlikely Ronald Reagan would have ever become president.

2

"I Shall Rise and Fight Again"

The 1976 Presidential Run

They man telephones, drive cars, run errands all for a candidate or a cause they believe in. And then when victory doesn't come, they stand with tears streaming down their cheeks as if somehow they hadn't done enough. You stand looking at those faces and hope you can say something to ease their grief and reward their dedication.

—Ronald Reagan, two weeks after his 1976
primary loss to President Gerald Ford

The most horrific moment of my political career began on Sunday, February 22, 1976, just two days before Ronald Reagan would face President Gerald Ford in the New Hampshire Republican primary. That day I was scheduled to catch a flight with Michael Deaver, Reagan's longtime aide. Deaver had met the governor just one year before my adventure to Reagan's home in Pacific Palisades. Yet by 1976 Mike and I had shared many a flight. In fact, Deaver had been with me the very first time Reagan and I flew together in 1969 on a tiny puddle jumper from Sacramento to San Diego. It was just the three of us and the pilot. As the airplane's propellers began to whirl before takeoff, I remember looking over at the governor. His eyes were closed and his head hung low. I nudged Deaver.

"Mike, is he sick?" I asked.

Deaver glanced over at Reagan and smiled. "Oh, don't worry about him, Dick. He always does that. He likes to pray for our safety and for Nancy before flying."

On this day seven years later, however, it was just Mike and me who would be flying. Since Deaver was in charge of scheduling travel, I hadn't given my itinerary a second thought. But looking over our flight schedule, I noticed what I thought was an error.

"Mike, why are we going to Illinois?" I asked.

"Because that's where the governor is, Dick," he replied.

And that's when the nightmare began.

One of the hardest things about being a pollster is that you often know bad news before anyone else. My latest poll, taken just one week before the New Hampshire primary, revealed that we were going to face a fierce battle. While we led Ford by four points, a week earlier it had been three times that margin and the undecided vote was running high. Worse, Ford was campaigning heavily in New Hampshire, and given the pomp and circumstance a president marshals when he comes rolling into town, I knew we were going to be in for the fight of our lives. A New Hampshire victory would depend on a strong ground game in the closing moments of the race, and I had said as much in my recent strategy memorandum to John Sears, Ronald Reagan's strategist during the 1976 campaign.

Sears is one of the most complex persons I've ever met. He is at once one of the most talented, undisciplined, manipulative, creative, and insecure people I've ever met. A lawyer by trade, his stint working in Richard Nixon's 1968 campaign had made him a favorite of the eastern media elite, a badge he wore proudly. Since Reagan's original California gang—Lyn Nofziger, Ed Meese, Stu Spencer, Michael Deaver, Marty Anderson, and myself—was comprised of westerners, Deaver had counseled that Sears would bring stature to Reagan's 1976 presidential campaign by allowing us to break out of the regional orbit and into the national scene.

On the surface, this seemed wise. No one could deny that Sears is bright and experienced. Moreover, wooing the eastern media would be essential for Reagan to position himself as a viable alternative to incumbent president Gerald Ford. But the problem with John Sears was that he didn't understand Ronald Reagan. Before I replaced Sears as Reagan's strategist in 1980, the Greatest Communicator described John best when he said, "I look him in the eye. He looks me in the tie!" What Reagan meant was that Sears viewed him more as a product than a person. Sears didn't seem to share our passion for Reagan's vision of what America could become under his leadership, and it wasn't always clear whose interests he was serving.

Still, I had to assume that John had his reasons for wanting to spend two days campaigning in Illinois before New Hampshire's first-in-the-nation primary. It made absolutely no sense to me, but I had to believe that he and Reagan had discussed some brilliant scenario under which being outside New Hampshire would actually help Reagan win. Yet the more I thought about it, the more worried I became. My memorandum had been clear: we only held a "whisper of a lead." Reagan's presence in the state would be, in my view, a critical component of achieving victory. But apparently Sears was of a different mind. He told me he felt swinging back to Reagan's home state two days before voters went to the polls was a good idea. Given my findings, for the life of me I couldn't understand why Reagan had agreed to do it.

But the problem with my logic was that it was based on the assumption that John Sears had actually *shown* the candidate my polling data and *discussed* my strategy memorandum.

After the stop in Illinois, on Monday, February 23, Reagan, Sears, and I sailed along in the campaign plane against a darkening New Hampshire sky. With the election less than twenty-four hours away, I could feel the wave of pre-game energy rolling through the cabin. Upon entering the aircraft, Reagan always liked to sit in the first or second row and preferred to be on the right side of the plane. This night he was seated in the first row by the window. More than halfway into the flight, Sears, who sat on the left side of the plane directly across from the candidate, looked over his left shoulder one row behind Reagan. When our eyes met, John motioned for me to move up to the seat next to his.

And that is when he dropped the bomb.

Sears confessed he had never shown the governor my numbers or analysis. That meant Reagan had no idea he was returning from a state he should never have visited in the first place. Worse, on the eve of the most important primary election of his career, the governor was entirely unaware of the slim lead he held against Ford just days prior to the voting, a lead that had evaporated with each hour wasted stumping in a state whose primary wasn't for another three weeks. And as if all that weren't bad enough, Sears had one last grenade to lob.

"Dick, I really think you should brief the governor about where he stands heading into tomorrow," he said.

It was a bit ironic to me that the man who had in a matter of forty-eight hours all but shattered Reagan's chances at victory was now asking me to be the carrier of bad news. In the darkened cabin of our campaign airplane sat a candidate filled with unfounded optimism, a foundation of hope no more stable than the clouds whisking past the windows of our plane.

I took a deep breath.

One of the recurring themes in my relationship with Ronald Reagan was that I was often the person who brought him the best and worst news. In addition to my own personal standards, another reason I never whitewashed my findings for Reagan was that he didn't want me to. The only thing worse than an unpopular leader is one who doesn't *know* he is unpopular. Don't misunderstand. Given the sometimes unpleasant findings, breaking bad news was always a difficult task. But then again, Reagan was never more energized than when confronting opposition. His enthusiasm would soar, his sights would focus, and his passion would stir. He was one of the few leaders I've ever known who actually derived *pleasure* from confrontation.

Some on the outer fringes thought that, since they had never personally heard me deliver bad news to Reagan, I sugarcoated findings. And they were right—they hadn't heard me deliver bad news, because my personal rule was to always discuss these matters privately with only Ronald Reagan and a very select group of his top advisers. For that reason, when there was a touchy matter to be handled, Nancy and others would often ask me to intervene. "He'll listen to you, Dick," Nancy would say.

Still, sliding across the aisle from Sears's side of the plane to Reagan's, I felt the same helpless, sinking feeling I had experienced the day before when Deaver informed me that we were traveling to Peoria, Illinois, instead of New Hampshire. I had known immediately that it was a costly strategic blunder. Then and there I vowed I would never allow another person to carry my numbers or strategic recommendations to Reagan. From that day forward I delivered them myself, often one-on-one.

But that did me little good now. In the time it took me to step from the left side of the plane to the right, a torrent of questions—all of them irrelevant at this point—flooded my mind: *Why had Sears never shown the candidate my numbers and memo? Was he setting me up to suffer the messenger's fate? Why hadn't Reagan protested the trip?*

I approached the candidate.

"Governor, mind if I join you for a moment?" I asked.

"Of course not, Dick," Reagan said.

"Governor, we need to talk about what will likely happen tomorrow," I said.

With the plane now entering its descent, I went over the polling data that had been kept hidden from Reagan. I explained how Ford had been closing in on us and that we enjoyed but a "whisper of a lead," as my earlier memorandum had cautioned. As I spoke, Reagan grew pensive and silent. I tried to leave room for an optimistic finish. After all, opinion research represents only a snapshot of events. But New Hampshire voters are an independent lot. Not being in their state slogging it out for their vote was likely to be interpreted as hubris, a slight voters seldom reward.

Breaking the news this way, hours before Reagan's electoral fate was to be decided, seemed almost cruel. His silence said everything. I had clearly delivered an emotional body blow, but he knew my heart and the depth of my loyalty to him. Cruising only a few thousand feet above Manchester, New Hampshire, I concluded my briefing and braced for his response.

He displayed no anger. Instead, he just sat quietly staring out the window of the plane. Although the silence probably lasted no more than two minutes, it felt like an eternity. I wondered what he was thinking. I wanted to say something. But what? What do you say in a moment like that? What do you say to a man grappling with the realization that his quest for the presidency—indeed, his entire political career—might be finished?

With his eyes fixed on the shimmering lights of the town below, Reagan said, "Well, Dick, I sure hope someone down there lights a candle for me."

Getting off the plane, I pulled Sears aside. I wanted to confront him directly.

"Why didn't you apprise the governor of what was happening?" I charged.

"The presence of the candidate would have taken away from

the manpower of the campaign volunteers and the get-out-the-vote efforts on the ground," he said.

"How could you *possibly* reach that conclusion?" I pressed.

"Because that's been my experience, Dick," Sears said.

We were in an unnecessarily precarious position, and everyone knew it. Because of its small size, New Hampshire yields only a handful of delegates. The true value of the state is its ability to generate momentum. John Sears's thinking all along seemed to be that a win in New Hampshire against Ford would pierce the incumbent's most credible political asset in the primary—the political leverage and pomp that always accompanies a president seeking reelection. The strategy was sound. The tactics were not.

I wish I could say my fears had been unfounded, my numbers inaccurate, and that Reagan pulled it out in the end. But he didn't. Instead, we suffered one of the closest defeats in New Hampshire history. When the 108,331 votes were tallied, President Ford edged us out by only 1,317 votes. Some in our own camp at the highest levels wanted Reagan to throw in the towel then and there. We had been summarily dismissed by just about everyone. Everyone, that is, except Ronald Reagan.

You have to understand: Reagan could be pugnacious. The more people called on him to quit, the more emboldened he became. I truly believe that the closeness of the New Hampshire loss made him more confident that all he needed was his message and the right moment. Given his communicative talents, I agreed. The night of the New Hampshire loss I decided to draw closer to Sears in the hopes of eliminating any more tactical debacles. That night, John and I stayed up until almost 3 A.M. poring over my most recent data. While studying my surveys alongside Reagan's speeches, I found what I hoped would be the "strategic hinge" that, if communicated effectively, just might swing the momentum back in our favor.

While campaigning in New Hampshire, Reagan had delivered a speech written by his talented speechwriter Peter Hannaford wherein he had argued that America needed a stronger, more aggressive foreign policy. Reagan criticized the Ford administration's intention to turn over ownership of the Panama Canal to the Panamanian government. A minor issue such as this might not seem like the rhetorical dynamite necessary to ignite victory. But issues are seldom what they appear. "Policy" is often little more than voters' values in disguise. What's more, issues are only as relevant as the symbolic meanings they produce.

For this reason, the question of who would control the Panama Canal packed a political punch. In the wake of Vietnam, many voters felt America lacked the respect and strength it once enjoyed. For those conservatives who considered America's entrance into Vietnam a mistake, control of the Panama Canal symbolized American autonomy and might. If Ronald Reagan could contrast his resolve to maintain ownership of the Panama Canal against Ford's position, I felt confident the governor's message could gain traction, something we needed desperately.

Out of money, tired, and feeling demoralized, Reagan had just lost five straight primaries. It was imperative that we win in North Carolina. But elections are strange. Sometimes you find that a loss in one state has sowed the seeds for victory in another. And so it was with the governor's performance in Florida—the primary preceding North Carolina—where Reagan had taped a hard-hitting speech based on the themes I had fleshed out during my all-nighter with Sears. The speech directly criticized Ford and his secretary of state, Henry Kissinger, for proposing to give away the Panama Canal. I still remember the "power line" from that speech. Standing at the lectern, Reagan would thunder, "We built it, we paid for it, it's ours, and we're going to keep it." The crowd roared with cheers. The speech struck the chord we had hoped it would.

And Tom Ellis, a North Carolina Republican Party activist, had agreed. After watching the Greatest Communicator deliver his speech, Ellis wanted to replay it on North Carolina television stations throughout the state. It was a risky proposition. The Reagan tape was almost a textbook example of how *not* to film a candidate. One rule in electoral politics is to never allow your candidate to become a "talking head." Talking heads, the assumption goes, are boring and turn people off, regardless of a candidate's eloquence. But Ronald Reagan had spent his whole life defying conventional wisdom. And besides, what did we have to lose? Ellis ran the tape. The results were astonishing.

We took North Carolina by ten points. His televised speech rekindled our electoral fire and ignited a blaze that spread west, allowing us to capture two of the biggest prizes in the primary: California and Texas. Reagan had been down for the count. He was now fighting back, landing devastating electoral blows against a sitting president. None of us had ever experienced a comeback like this. The momentum was suddenly on our side, and it was Reagan's words that were making the difference. So much so that weeks after the North Carolina victory our campaign coffers were replenished with an influx of over $1.5 million. We had gained ground, and Ronald Reagan was proven correct. He would take the fight all the way to the Republican National Convention.

On August 19, 1976, Republicans, some wearing garish, elephant-clad regalia, oversized campaign buttons, and hats only a conventioneer could love, bustled about the convention floor at the Kemper Arena in Kansas City, Missouri. Back then there was still reason to bustle. These were the days when national conventions actually decided a party's presidential ticket, days when suspense and excitement were less the work of creative convention planners and more the result of genuine intra-party battles played out before an anxious electorate. If onlookers were hoping for a close, climactic drama, none were disappointed. It was to be one of the GOP's closest fights in modern history.

From our corner, that the race was tight was a major accomplishment. But Ronald Reagan wasn't running for a second-place finish or a spot on the national ticket as vice president. And speaking of running mates, Sears, having surveyed the terrain, determined Reagan needed to launch a Hail Mary pass by announcing his vice presidential selection early. John tapped liberal Republican senator Richard Schweiker from Pennsylvania. But ultimately, this only served to annoy many of the conservative delegates on whom we depended. They felt betrayed, as if the spokesman for conservatism had traded his core principles for political expediency.

In the end, of the 2,257 delegates who cast ballots, 117 votes was all that separated Reagan from the party's presidential nomination. That should have been cause for celebration. A sitting president hadn't lost his party's nomination in almost a century. Yet sometimes losing by a razor-thin margin is harder than losing in a landslide. We had all ridden an emotional roller coaster for months, spending nights in cheap motels and stealing sleep on buses, couches, and airplanes whenever we could. So when the final tally was announced from the rostrum, the whole team felt demoralized. For me, however, the sting of defeat was to be short-lived. In fact, I know the exact moment it ended. In the midst of his acceptance speech, Ford looked up at our skybox and invited Ronald Reagan to join him on the platform to say a few words.

"Come on down, Ron," Ford said.

The whole thing was a surprise. None of us knew Ford would do it—or that Reagan would agree to participate—until just before it happened. Ford, for whom I had previously worked, was a smart politician and a fine human being. But it is my nagging assumption that the Ford advisers counseled the president to launch the gambit because they, like some Americans, assumed Ronald Reagan could only deliver a speech when he had a script in hand. Having him falter live before a national television audience would ensure that Reagan would no longer be a threat.

There was also a second reason for Ford to invite our candidate onstage. Although he had been extremely unhappy about Reagan's initial decision to challenge him in the primary, Ford knew voters needed to see a unified Republican Party. Shoring up any fissures was key. Having Reagan join him onstage would send a strong visual message of unity. So Ford at first sent speechwriter Bryce Harlow—who, incidentally, had written many of President Eisenhower's most famous speeches—up to our skybox. Bryce said President Ford wanted Reagan to join him on the platform. At first, the governor was opposed to the idea. He felt it was Ford's night to shine. He didn't want to be seen as trying to upstage the nominee. But Bryce persisted. He said the president wanted Reagan to join him. The governor agreed on the condition that Ford invite him from the stage to come join him. If he was invited from the platform, Reagan would do it. Harlow disappeared from our skybox before returning with confirmation: Ford would ask the governor to "Come on down."

Talk about pressure! If you've ever had to give a formal speech, you know the feeling. Now imagine that you've had no time to prepare, no time to practice, and that you have to deliver a speech before a live audience of thousands and a televised audience of tens of millions! It was as if everything in his life before that point—Hollywood, *GE Theater*, being governor of California—had been preparing him for that moment. Indeed, it had.

Here was Reagan, seemingly the happiest of political warriors, making his way to the podium. I don't care if you were the biggest Jerry Ford fan, a yellow dog Democrat, or just a casual political observer, you couldn't help but feel for Reagan the emotion all Americans do for an underdog whose fingertips graze victory. I can tell you that the feeling is magnified when you work for a candidate in whom you believe deeply.

So, as the crowd's applause propelled Reagan toward the stage, I was hurting for Nancy and the governor. He was intensely competitive, and she didn't like to see her husband disappointed. I knew how hard they had both worked and fought and hoped. But his outward image told a different story. He believed what most men born of our generation believed: pain was something to be hidden, a pill best swallowed in secret.

After being hustled through a network of tunnels and doors, Reagan appeared onstage. Standing there amid the raucous cheers and clapping hands, he was smiling. But anyone who really knew him understood his smile was more for us than for him.

Since President Ford's invitation was a surprise, it suddenly dawned on me that the governor might not have a prepared speech. My eyes darted to Reagan's hands and then down to his jacket pocket. His familiar packet of four-by-six-inch note cards wrapped in a rubber band was nowhere in sight. Since I frequently helped craft and strategize the framing of his speeches, I knew this meant he had absolutely *nothing* formally prepared. Worse, he would have to improvise his speech after having just been dealt the knockout punch. Like everyone else watching, I wondered what he would say. Reagan, it turns out, was asking himself the same question. As they were being escorted by Secret Service agents to the stage, he told Nancy, "I don't know what to say." It was a rare moment of true political suspense. She told him not to worry. "You'll think of something," she said. And he did.

After thanking the president, Mrs. Ford, and convention-goers, Reagan delivered an impromptu speech that left many Republicans wondering whether they had just made a colossal mistake. This wasn't your obligatory concession speech. In fact, the address didn't have anything to do with the candidate or even his supporters. This was a speech about the topic for which Ronald Reagan was most passionate—the future.

People who think conservatives are stuck in the past don't

understand men like Reagan. And maybe that's partly our fault. When you hear any of us who worked closely with him speak we will often say things like, "Reagan was a big-picture leader," or, "He believed in large, overarching goals and ideas." We do him a disservice when we say such things. Ronald Reagan didn't just see the "big picture." He stretched the frame, widened the lens, and believed life was best viewed from a panoramic perspective. His speech in Kansas City was powerful precisely because it defied the dictates of the moment. Instead of looking back, it looked forward. Instead of focusing on him, it focused on America. It was, in a word, *selfless*.

Here is some of what he said that night:

I had an assignment the other day. Someone asked me to write a letter for a time capsule that is going to be opened in Los Angeles a hundred years from now, on our Tricentennial. It sounded like an easy assignment. They suggested I write something about the problems and issues today. I set out to do so, riding down the coast in an automobile, looking at the blue Pacific out on one side and the Santa Ynez Mountains on the other, and I couldn't help but wonder if it was going to be that beautiful a hundred years from now as it was on that summer day. . . .

Let your own minds turn to that task. You are going to write for people a hundred years from now who know all about us. We know nothing about them. We don't know what kind of a world they will be living in.

And suddenly I thought to myself, if I write of the problems, they will be the domestic problems the President spoke of here tonight; the challenges confronting us, the erosion of freedom that has taken place under Democratic rule in this country, the invasion of private rights, the controls and restrictions on the vitality of the great free economy that we enjoy. These are our challenges that we must meet.

And then again, there is that challenge of which he spoke that we live in a world in which the great powers have poised and aimed at each other horrible missiles of destruction, nuclear weapons that can—in a matter of minutes—arrive at each other's country and destroy, virtually, the civilized world we live in.

And suddenly it dawned on me; those who would read this letter a hundred years from now will know whether those missiles were fired. They will know whether we met our challenge. Whether they have the freedoms that we have known up until now will depend on what we do here.

Will they look back with appreciation and say, "Thank God for those people in 1976 who headed off that loss of freedom, who kept us now one hundred years later free, who kept our world from nuclear destruction?"

And if we failed, they probably won't get to read the letter at all because it spoke of individual freedom, and they won't be allowed to talk of that or read of it.

This is our challenge; and this is why here in this hall tonight, better than we have ever done before, we have got to quit talking to each other and about each other and go out and communicate to the world that we may be fewer in numbers than we have ever been, but we carry the message they are waiting for.

We must go forth from here united, determined that what a great general said a few years ago is true: There is no substitute for victory.

The words of his from-the-heart address thrust our minds into the future. The speech challenged listeners to connect actions with consequences, words to deeds, emotions with logic, and dreams to reality. It had nothing to do with elections or candidates or campaigns. Those are small things. This wasn't a speech about small things. This was a speech about the *biggest* things. It was about our children, our humanity, our very existence. Few things matter more.

After the speech, I started replaying the governor's words in my mind. I had the strangest feeling I had heard parts of it before. But, for the life of me, I couldn't remember where. Finally I remembered. A few days before we arrived in Kansas City, Reagan and I had been chatting while riding to an event. In the course of our conversation he told me about the time capsule assignment and how the world might be viewed in the future. As he did, I sensed he was scanning my response. It was something I had seen him do often. He was pre-testing speech material. Reagan had started the practice during his days as a pitchman for General Electric. He would switch up anecdotes and gestures from audience to audience in order to find the most potent rhetorical weaponry.

It was, of course, the best way to hone a message. Sort of a one-man focus group! I've often speculated that part of his intrigue with survey research stemmed from his days field-testing material before audiences. As every public speaker knows, analyzing one's audience is a critical component of making sure a message makes a positive impact. And one audience Reagan knew better than most was his California supporters.

Following his defeat at the 1976 Republican Convention in Kansas City, Reagan would give one final impromptu speech, a speech that in my mind had done the unimaginable: it had eclipsed his earlier performance onstage with Jerry Ford. With roughly 250 members of the California delegation and those of us who were privileged to serve him as his audience, the defeated candidate stood on a little platform in the austere surroundings of a bare basement room of the Kemper Arena. There, he told us what we needed and wanted to hear—this wasn't an end, it was a beginning. At one point, Reagan touched each of our hearts and hopes by reciting the words of an Irish ballad: "I will lay me down and bleed a while. Though I am wounded, I am not slain. I shall rise and fight again."

The moment was electric. Some cried, others smiled, and I suspect most of us did a little of both. Someone recently asked me if there was a time I was proudest of Ronald Reagan and this moment came to mind immediately. On the surface, this response might seem a little odd. After all, it was the only time Reagan ever tasted electoral defeat in his political career. But that is why it was so revealing. It's easy to be gracious in victory. Facing defeat is much harder, particularly when the stakes are so high and the race so close. Instead of being bitter, Reagan was determined, optimistic, and inspiring. To have been there to witness it in person was a blessing I don't think I'll ever forget.

A few weeks after the Republican Convention and Reagan's inspirational rhetoric, I received a phone call. The Reagans wanted the inner circle to join them at their home in Pacific Palisades—the place of my first meeting with the governor—for a luncheon in early September. When I arrived, Mike Deaver, John Sears, Peter Hannaford, Charlie Black, and Jim Lake were all there. We all mended fences over a delicious lunch complete with shrimp salad. During the meeting, Reagan sent distinct signals that this soldier wasn't interested in just fading away—at least not yet. He wanted to remain active in the issues upon which he had built his career. So the governor decided to campaign vigorously in twenty states on Ford's behalf. Still, although he never directly told me so that day, I knew in my heart of hearts that were Ford to lose, Reagan would be open to another run for the White House.

But a win in 1980 would make him the oldest person in U.S. history ever elected president. For this reason, some among the old California gang thought the window might have closed on Reagan's chances. I ran surveys to see if his age would be a major issue. Voters sent mixed signals. To look at him, Reagan appeared spry, youthful, and full of vitality. Indeed, he was. But when people were told how old he was, red flags shot up for some. Regardless, I interpreted the luncheon as Reagan laying his marker down. It was his way of reaching out and letting us know that the old gang might soon ride again.

And we would.

Just as he promised in the basement of the Kemper Arena, it wouldn't be long before Reagan would make his return. In 1980, Ronald Reagan would rise and fight again.

3

"Are You Better Off . . . ?"

The 1980 Landslide

We are too great a nation to limit ourselves to small dreams. We are not, as some would have us believe, doomed to an inevitable decline. . . . We have every right to dream heroic dreams.

—Ronald Reagan, First Inaugural Address,
January 20, 1981

I remember the exact moment I knew Ronald Reagan could beat Jimmy Carter.

The date was July 15, 1979. By then, America was already careening toward optimism's edge when President Carter decided to step on the accelerator by delivering the most important speech of his political life, the infamous "Malaise" speech. The word "malaise" never actually appeared in his remarks. Carter's strategist and pollster, Patrick H. Caddell, had used the term to describe American discontent in a private memorandum advising Carter to deliver the speech. Originally, his address had been titled "A Crisis of Confidence." Yet, far from calming any crisis, Carter's oration created one—for himself! The immediate public response to the speech was actually somewhat favorable. But the instant I heard it I knew Carter had stepped on a strategic land mine. Indeed, once his rhetoric bounced its way through the media echo chamber, views quickly turned negative.

Carter seemed to be suggesting that *the people* were the problem and that *government* was the solution. Reagan believed the reverse. "Government isn't the solution," Reagan would later declare. "Government is the problem." Two leaders' visions could not have been more inversely related. And these differences were most clearly on display when each man communicated.

What Ronald Reagan understood was that you cannot not communicate. That's not a misprint. Go back and read it again. There is no way a human being can do anything without in some way communicating a message—verbally or nonverbally. Now, a person might not *intend* to send a certain message, but that is the harsh reality of communication: received meaning and original intent don't always work in tandem.

President Carter, for example, obviously didn't *intend* to insult Americans by blaming them for the woes that many believed his administration had created, such as high taxes, an energy crisis, skyrocketing inflation, and a rudderless foreign policy. But how else were voters to feel about a president who spoke about American greatness in the past tense? What were citizens to think about a president who charged dourly that, "In a nation that *was* [emphasis mine] proud of hard work, strong families, close-knit communities and our faith in God, too many of us now tend to worship self-indulgence and consumption"? Despite his sincerity and affable nature, Carter was actually pointing the finger at voters for failed citizenship, not at himself for failed leadership! When I heard it I about fell out of my chair.

Americans expect presidents to provide strong leadership. Moreover, we are an innately optimistic people. One of the great currents that rushes through U.S. history is the belief that Americans can accomplish anything if we just work hard enough. That was the Reagan philosophy. If someone had handed Reagan a speech like Carter's he would have crumpled it up. All but begging Americans to "say something good about our country," as Carter had, was an indictment of his inability to devise a bold vision and turn it into a reality. What's more, the president's speech was riddled with pessimism, and pessimism pierces American presidencies.

Reagan, on the other hand, didn't accept pessimism, especially when it was directed toward America. It defied his nature. One of his favorite jokes that I heard him spin many times illustrates this point.

The parents of two brothers—one an incurable pessimist and the other an incurable optimist—took their sons to see a doctor in the hopes of curing the boys of their respective conditions. The physician started with the young pessimist. He took the boy into a room brimming with a mountain of new toys. "These are all yours," the doctor said. Immediately, the young pessimist burst into tears. "What's wrong?" his parents asked. "If I play with the toys," the boy sobbed, "surely they will all break and be ruined."

Next, the doctor tried his hand with the young optimist. Instead of toys, the doctor took his patient into a room filled with a mountain of horse dung. "This is for you," the doctor told him. With that, the boy smiled so wide he could have eaten a banana sideways. Excited, he raced to the top of the mountain of manure, where, with his bare hands, he began digging into the pungent heap. Baffled, the doctor and the parents looked at one another quizzically. "Son," the father asked, "what in heaven's name do you think you're doing?"

"Well," the boy replied, "with all this horse dung, I figure there's got to be a pony in there *somewhere!*"

The problem with Carter's "Malaise" speech was that it was all about broken toys. Worse for him, he was up against a man who believed in the unbridled potential of America. And that is why, watching Carter deliver his gloom-and-doom speech, I knew Reagan could win. Carter had begged a central question: "If, Mr. President, things are as bad as you say—indeed, if we have reached a 'Crisis of Confidence'—then why, pray tell, have you not done anything to fix it?" And so, the logic followed: if Carter thinks America is in real trouble and offers nothing but philosophical platitudes, why would voters want another four more years of failed leadership?

They wouldn't.

Carter's strategic miscue had revealed a president without a plan. Even those who accepted the malaise thesis saw that he offered no solution. He might not have meant to come across that way, but that was how he was perceived. And in politics, perception is everything. Whatever the realities about our elected leaders—negative or positive—they are almost irrelevant in predicting public acceptance or rejection. For better or worse, not what is, but what appears to be, often determines the image of public figures.

When it came to perceptions about Reagan, the governor's critics liked to say the image of Ronald Reagan was divorced from the reality of Ronald Reagan. The Carter campaign was determined to make Reagan look dumb, dangerous, and a distorter of facts. Others, particularly those in the media, charged that Reagan was more interested in creating powerful pictures than sound policies. These characterizations were unfair and silly, of course. Yet it is true that he understood the important role symbolic communication plays in the American presidency. He knew that symbols often build or destroy administrations. Carter's "Malaise" speech proved that. But it was another Democratic president, Franklin Delano Roosevelt, who had taught Reagan that symbols could be used to bring uplift as well.

I remember once in March 1982, Nancy, the president, and I were riding on Air Force One. During the flight Reagan and I talked a great deal about how one of his heroes, President Franklin Delano Roosevelt, had kept hope alive in the direst of times. Reagan said that the reason FDR was able to keep spirits bright was that he was doing things that would not have been done before, such as establishing the CCC camps and the WPA. But more than that, Reagan explained how FDR kept the American flag front and center in the minds of citizens lacking hope.

"You know, Dick, President Roosevelt used to march the troops in Chicago. But he didn't march them down Michigan Avenue [one of the city's more prominent locations] but down State Street where those who slept in doorways with papers would be sure to see them."

Reagan knew that a president's every move has the potential to communicate meaning in powerful ways, either implicitly or explicitly. When a leader enters the arena of public opinion, to Reagan, miscommunication is simply not an option. That means being prepared to the hilt. And that is partly where I came in. Engaging in excessive planning remains a charge of which I am almost always found guilty. I've traced this aspect of my personality all the way back to the Boy Scouts, of all places! As a young man I was taught that if you are always prepared you will never have anything to fear, and I believed it. Although that advice hasn't always been borne out, for the most part, I've found it sure beats the alternative.

Following Reagan's defeat in 1976, my disdain for uncertainty had only intensified. I vowed that the governor's 1980 run for the White House would be different. Determined to tilt the odds in certainty's favor, I decided that something major must be done. As early as 1978, my firm, then named Decision Making Information, started construction on a new information weapon, a massive computer system I called the

Political Information System, or PINS for short. PINS combined every quantitative, qualitative, institutional, and historical data source available. The system was like a massive computerized chessboard. It allowed me to simulate, or "war game," how Reagan's rhetorical "moves," such as his media and campaign tours, might influence the outcome of the 1980 presidential election. Altogether, it took us about two and half years to build.

For example, PINS allowed us to make assumptions about the profile of the electorate: Who was likely to turn out? How were various constituencies likely to vote? To what extent was an issue relevant to voters and which candidate perceptually "owned" that issue? Then we would run a series of "What if?" questions, knowing well in advance what Reagan's positions were. We weren't running the simulation to determine a "best position" on the issues. After all, much to his critics' chagrin, Reagan's stance on issues hadn't changed in decades, so using PINS to gauge popular policies would have been a major waste of time and resources. Instead, the system helped determine where we were vulnerable, as well as where we were strong. But most importantly, PINS gave us insight into how best to allocate our then scarce resources. For example, it could help us determine where the candidate should spend his time and where we should purchase advertising on radio and television. In sum, PINS allowed us to enhance Reagan's probability of securing at least the golden 270 electoral votes and the presidency.

Honestly, PINS was a bit of a gamble. Nothing quite like it had been tried before. Originally I had envisioned a system that would assist the campaign strategist in making better decisions. I had no idea that that person would soon be me. Nevertheless, I'm glad I had PINS at my disposal, because I ended up using it every single day of the campaign.

But at the outset of the 1980 presidential election, no one needed a computer to realize that a Reagan victory was far from assured. In fact, you could even say it was unlikely. Before the governor could go toe to toe with Jimmy Carter he would first have to gain the Republican Party's nomination in a fiercely contested primary. As before, Reagan's words would reshape the electoral landscape.

With Reagan's 1976 New Hampshire primary defeat still fresh in our minds, everyone involved in the campaign was committed to not let history repeat itself. The inner circle had been reassembled, and John Sears was back at the helm. Initially, things appeared to be running smoothly. But by January 1980, the campaign had veered off course and into troubled waters.

First, there were the serial firings. Sears seemed to have his sights set on eliminating a good portion of the California gang. My dear friend Lyn Nofziger, Reagan's gubernatorial and campaign press secretary, was the first to be picked off. Nofziger and Sears had never gotten along. John let Lyn tie his own noose by putting Nofziger in charge of a daunting task—fundraising. Lyn is the first person to admit he is not a natural fund-raiser. So when he failed to reach the benchmark numbers, Sears had the cover he needed to cut him.

Next came Mike Deaver. Mike's dismissal at the Reagans' home in Pacific Palisades had been particularly ugly. Reagan was furious over how Sears, Lake, and Black had forced Deaver out of the campaign. Through the years, Mike and I had occasionally found ourselves at swords' points, but he was always one of us, and he remains a good friend to this day. Thankfully, Deaver would return. Yet at the time, this seemed highly unlikely.

Sears's next hatchet appeared to have Ed Meese's—one of my best friends—name written on it, and that is when we all decided enough was enough. Perhaps it would have been different for some in our camp—although I seriously doubt it— if the campaign had been humming along. But on January 21,

1980, the day of the Iowa caucuses, Sears began making the case for his own release. In what had become an eerie replay of Reagan's 1976 New Hampshire defeat, amazingly, the governor had lost the Iowa caucuses. It was like sitting through a rerun of a bad movie you hadn't wanted to see the first time. Just as before, Sears had pulled Reagan out too early. And, just as before, Reagan lost narrowly. This time the loss came at the hands of George H. W. Bush. Bush beat us by 2,182 votes, giving him something he called the "Big Mo," as in "momentum."

Before she became treasurer of the United States and the CNN media star she is today, Bay Buchanan served as our able head of finance. Bay remembers that the campaign was so bad off financially that, excepting staff salaries, it couldn't cover its own expenses. We were flat broke. Worse, people were beginning to get worried that Reagan might be ripe for a political upset.

And that's why on February 22, four days before the New Hampshire primary, Nancy was livid. She called me and said that something needed to be done, and now. Like the rest of us, she felt Sears was hurting Reagan's chances at victory. So she asked Nevada senator Paul Laxalt and me to confront the governor about letting Sears go.

Despite John's mismanagement, I didn't relish the call. For all his mistakes, Sears was a brilliant man, a person from whom I had learned much. But everyone knew his departure was in the governor's best interests. When Laxalt and I called to express the campaign's consensus, Reagan understood completely. As it turned out, the candidate shared many of the same concerns himself. Several years later, Reagan would say that he sensed Sears had grown jealous of the Californians' closeness to him.

Regardless, letting Sears, Lake, and Black go just days before the first-in-the-nation primary would be tricky. On the one hand, if Reagan were to lose New Hampshire, having fired

Sears in the wake of defeat would make the candidate appear a sore loser and smack of sour grapes. If, on the other hand, Reagan fired John before voters went to the polls, the shake-up could stir the media hornet's nest, thereby raising doubts in the minds of some voters.

From whatever angle you looked at it, Reagan was still firing people, and that was something he always hated to do. Honestly, I think his inability to let people go—even when he knew they were hurting him politically—went back to his days living through the Great Depression. Having witnessed his neighbors and family struggle to make ends meet, Reagan knew the value of a job. He understood how a man's pride and ability to feed his family were tied to his work. I saw him display that kind of caring and humanity throughout his career. It was a part of him I respected deeply. Yet even he had come to the realization that the damage had become too costly to ignore. So, after huddling up, the campaign decided it would be best to cut Sears on the day of the New Hampshire primary.

Before Sears's departure, however, Reagan would put on a rhetorical performance that would go down as a one of his more memorable oratorical moments. It happened at the Nashua, New Hampshire, Republican presidential debate. The local newspaper, the *Nashua Telegraph*, had hosted the event, but since Federal Election Commission laws prevented them from covering the cost, our campaign picked up the tab.

The newspaper wanted a two-person debate between Reagan and Bush. Not surprisingly, the Bush camp favored this arrangement too. By cutting a seven-man race down to two, Bush could instantly increase his stature as a candidate. We weren't about to play into his hands, however. After the earlier debate in Manchester, New Hampshire, my data revealed a clear and convincing finding: multicandidate debates over-whelmingly favored Reagan.

In the run-up to the Nashua debate it was obvious that both the Bush campaign and the *Nashua Telegraph* were determined to keep the other Republican candidates off the stage—literally. But since we were paying for the event, Reagan decided to invite the other candidates as his personal guests. When everyone arrived at the high school gymnasium in Nashua, only two chairs sat on the stage. When Reagan and Bush sat down, the other four candidates—Bob Dole, Phil Crane, John Anderson, and Howard Baker—huddled up behind Reagan and stood awkwardly onstage. Not knowing what to do, Bush sat silently. The audience had no clue as to what was happening. Shouts of impatience began filling the air. And that is when Reagan leaned into his microphone to explain the situation.

But before the governor could finish, Jon Breen, the *Nashua Telegraph*'s executive editor and the debate moderator, ordered the sound technician to "turn Mr. Reagan's microphone off." With that, Reagan boomed, "Mr. Green, I *paid* for this microphone!" The crowd went wild. It mattered little that Reagan had mispronounced Breen's name. The moment had communicated the governor's decisiveness and strength.

Today, Reagan's line has become a legend of political campaign history. Many have cast it as the deciding factor that clinched the Republican primary. While that version of events may make for compelling political lore, in actuality, the Nashua debate had relatively little impact on New Hampshire voters. For one, the debate was not televised. Other than the two thousand or so viewers who packed the Nashua High School gymnasium, no one witnessed it live. The ripple effect from news media replaying the clip helped. But the real shift in momentum had occurred after the Manchester debate that was held only a few days prior, not the Nashua debate. Still, watching the footage today it is easy to understand why political junkies like to ignore this important distinction. The Nashua debate produced the kind of moment candidates and strategists dream of—the chance to bottle strength and command in a seven-second sound bite.

The Sunday after the debate I called the governor to tell him the good news. Reagan answered the phone.

"Are you sitting down, Governor? Our latest numbers have you leading Bush by seventeen points and soaring." When Reagan repeated the numbers aloud for the other campaign staff in the room to hear, a cheer rang out.

On February 26, 1980, Reagan garnered 51 percent of New Hampshire votes in a seven-man field. The next closest candidate was Bush who had only garnered 22 percent of the vote. It was a watershed event. He had finally redeemed himself from his '76 defeat.

Another significant event occurred that day, too. Just as planned, Reagan released Sears, Lake, and Black. I suspect the three men had sensed a change was imminent, but I was relieved when Reagan reported that they all took it in stride.

The shake-up in the campaign structure had raised important questions about who would fill their shoes. Reagan soon answered them. Bill Casey was named campaign manager. Ed Meese was put in charge of policy planning. And as for the campaign's strategist, Reagan pulled me aside and said, "As you know, we're making some important changes in the campaign. Dick, I'd like you to be in charge of strategy from here on out." I thanked him for the vote of confidence and told him how honored I was that he had asked.

But as soon as Reagan tapped me to serve as the campaign's chief strategist, my mind began kicking into overdrive. Lying in bed that night, I couldn't sleep. One set of numbers kept glowing in my mind—56–28. That was the percentage of those who considered themselves Democrats versus Republicans. Conventional wisdom among political professionals held that party identification was one of the strongest indicators of voting behavior. But if that were the case, even if we won the Republican primary, Reagan would have little chance of defeating incumbent president Jimmy Carter in the general election. How was Reagan going to persuade Democrats to vote for him? The answer to this riddle helped me unlock one of the Greatest Communicator's most treasured secrets. Yet this revelation wouldn't come until just before the 1980 Republican National Convention in Detroit, Michigan.

In the interim, the 1980 presidential campaign gave Reagan and me a chance to bolster our friendship and trust. Having run dozens of campaigns through the years, I have come to the conclusion that political contests dramatically impact the relationships between advisers and candidates. There is just something about grown men being stuck on buses, put up in cheap motels, and eating bad food together that draws them closer or rips them apart. For Reagan and me, campaigning forged stronger bonds. But on the road to winning the White House, like all relationships, we had our fair share of awkward and uncomfortable moments. Looking back, though, I wouldn't trade a single one. Not even the time that Ronald Reagan lied to me.

It only happened once, but the lie revolved around the hardest thing Ronald Reagan ever asked me to do during our thirty-six-year relationship—buy Nancy an anniversary card on his behalf.

On March 4, 1980, the governor was involved in a series of lengthy meetings and didn't have the time to pick out an anniversary card for Nancy. Now, if you've read Nancy's book of love letters, you know that Reagan was an incurable romantic. Sure, from time to time, he might ignore details. But forget doing something special for Nancy? Never.

Between meetings, Reagan pulled me aside and looked me square in the eyes. "Dick, I hate to ask you to do this, but I need a favor. You booked me so solid today I don't think there's any way I'll have time to break free. I need you to buy Nancy an anniversary card for me. Just pick out a nice one and I'll pay you back."

Reimbursement was my *last* concern.

"Oh, I don't know. I just don't think I . . ."

"Dick, just do me this favor, please?"

What was I going to say? No?

"Well . . . okay . . . okay. Is there any particular type of card that you'd like me to purchase?"

Grinning, he put his hand on my shoulder and said, "I know you'll pick a good one."

Great! I thought. *Make this assignment a barometer of my judgment!* Ask me to devise a national presidential campaign strategy? No problem. Need counsel on how to build support for the tax bill? I've got you covered. Need help framing your acceptance speech? My pleasure. Pick out an anniversary card for your wife?

I was officially in uncharted territory.

I don't get anxious.

I was anxious.

And here's why. Quick: when you think of all the places in the world to find a sentimental, loving, heartfelt card for your sweetheart, what is the first place that comes to mind? That's right! You guessed it. None other than that bastion of all things romantic: Washington's very own Dulles International Airport! That's where we were when he asked, and there was no time to go elsewhere.

Lest one think purchasing greeting cards at Dulles a good idea, let's just say the selection leaves much to be desired. I should know. I went through every single card the little newsstand kiosk sold—twice. I'd pick one up and flick it open: *No, that one's too sappy.* Then another. *Totally wrong. Too suggestive.* And another. *Not romantic enough.* I must have gone back and forth a dozen times. *This is crazy*, I said to myself, *Just pick one!* So I took my first choice, which is to say the *least* awful of the lot, up to the cashier and bought it before slipping it into my briefcase.

When Reagan was finished with his meetings, I sheepishly unveiled the card.

"As you might imagine, Governor, there wasn't much of a selection. I looked at every anniversary card they had. But it won't hurt my feelings if this isn't what you had in mind."

As I handed him the card, I paused before releasing it. "Governor, just one more thing. Would you please not tell Nancy I picked it out?"

Reagan smiled and said, "I won't, Dick. I won't. And listen, thanks again. I appreciate it."

Well, I forgot about the whole incident until a few days later when Nancy met up with us on the campaign trail. As soon as I saw her, I remembered the card. As soon as she saw me, she did too. Her smile let me know something was up.

"It's so good to see you. I've been meaning to thank you, Dick."

"You're welcome. But for what?" I asked.

"For my anniversary card, that's what for! Ronnie told me the whole story. I think he felt a little guilty. He told me you picked out his card for me."

This was, of course, vintage Reagan. He could never keep a secret from her. It was one of the things that made their marriage so special. To be sure, like any husband and wife, they had their spats. But theirs was truly a marriage based on a mutual passion and friendship. It was an incredible romance that never wavered. Indeed, in the painful last days of the president's battle with Alzheimer's, Nancy's devotion and love for her husband were at their strongest.

Someone once said of relationships, "The immature lover says, 'I love you because I need you.' But the mature lover says, 'I need you because I love you.'" Ronald and Nancy Reagan's love was mature.

Equally mature was Reagan's mastery of the art of leadership, a word often used and little understood. Leadership, after all, is not raw power. It is not even authority. I define leadership as the power to persuade in ways that change people's lives.

Although Reagan clinched the GOP primary victory convincingly, beating Jimmy Carter in the general election would require a strategy designed to highlight Reagan's leadership by showcasing what he did best—communicate to voters a set of commonly shared values.

With that idea as my guide, I mapped out a 176-page campaign plan. Journalists later dubbed it "The Black Book." The document provided the whole framework for Ronald Reagan's 1980 presidential campaign. It was designed to achieve a critical component of effective political strategy: coordinating the various layers of the campaign around a core set of assumptions and themes. In so doing, the Black Book provided Reagan and his inner circle with a blueprint for electoral victory.

It also included an analysis of the ways the election could be lost. This was important. As Reagan always maintained, nothing is more detrimental to a campaign than overconfidence. I remember how uneasy he would get days before an election when I would project victory. Wisely, he had never forgotten that famous picture of a smiling Harry Truman—whom Reagan had once campaigned for—holding up a copy of the *Chicago Daily Tribune*, whose erroneous poll projections had prompted the newspaper to print an advance copy with a headline that shouted: "Dewey Defeats Truman." That image is seared into the psyche of any good pollster. And in that spirit of caution, the Black Book warned that Carter would be a formidable opponent.

Another key objective of the Black Book involved devising Reagan's overarching campaign theme. As Reagan's handwritten letters and radio scripts reveal, he understood that good communication involved crafting short messages marked by clarity. But the frenetic pace of modern presidential campaigns forces candidates to delegate the responsibility of crafting communications to their advisers. So when framing his campaign theme, I tried to follow Reagan's lead by distilling our message down into just two phrases—"Strong Leader" and "A

Problem-solving Country." I explained that the national mood would have serious strategic implications, and that presidents are elected on the basis of the voters' expectations about the candidate's ability to exert strong, decisive, able, and popular leadership in light of the prevailing political mood of the country. In 1980, the national mood was disenchanted and pessimistic, and not significantly different than it was before President Carter took office four years earlier. Jimmy Carter had failed to provide the moral and political leadership needed to restore the country and give it its proper bearings.

I concluded that the "strategic implication of the crisis of confidence in the 1980 presidential campaign is not whether there is a crisis or even how upset Americans actually are. The essence of presidential leadership," I continued, "is to establish the expectation that the president will take courageous stands on pressing national issues, will insist that government respond to the will of the people, will stimulate the private sectors of the society, will perform, and reaffirm the nation's highest purposes. The result will be less uncertainty about what the future portends. Leadership is the ability to enlarge men's vision about the future and give them expectations of a less uncertain and more gratifying future."

Journalists may have given the Black Book a mysterious name, but the "secret" to Reagan's victory lay with the candidate's ability to communicate. Heading into the Republican National Convention in Detroit, our greatest goal was to let Reagan be Reagan. That meant making sure his convention acceptance speech—the biggest speech of his political career up to that point—captured the depth and breadth of his vision and his ability to communicate. Indeed, Reagan's acceptance speech revealed one of the secrets of his communicative success. It allowed him to communicate a set of commonly shared values. Over a lifetime spent communicating to the public, he had developed a rhetorical method best summed up in six simple words: *Persuade through reason. Motivate through emotion.*

What put Reagan in a league of his own was his intuitive but sure understanding that values are the strategic linchpins of effective persuasion. I define values as the measures by which individuals determine the worth or importance of matters of concern in their lives. For example, "freedom" is a value. If a person cherishes freedom, that value becomes the yardstick by which he or she can measure the importance of relevant public policies. A president might argue that a given military action is necessary to protect our "freedom." The presence of that value communicates that the speaker treasures an insight that exists within the individual members of his or her audience. Put another way, if persuasive communication skills are precious jewels, then values are the showcase used to display them.

Once shared values have been identified, leaders must show they embrace those values in their own lives and successfully embed them in their policies and programs. Reagan knew that the best way to do that was to *persuade through reason and motivate through emotion.* It took me years to fully appreciate the meaning of those words. However, my time with Reagan and the countless leadership studies I conducted on his behalf allowed me to probe the depths of his communication style. Before I explain how Reagan's rhetorical method worked, let me give you a little background.

Around the time Reagan left office as governor of California, I decided to investigate a peculiar pattern in his level of public support that went all the way back to that first study I conducted for him in 1968. Among Democratic voters (particularly Catholics and blue-collar workers), he almost always received five to seven points more than would typically be expected for a candidate expressing similar policy preferences. You may have heard people talk about the "Reagan Democrats." That's simply the term some journalists and commentators used to refer to this phenomenon. To this day, many scholars and political observers believe the Reagan Democrats were the product of Ronald Reagan's charm and charisma. For a time, I too thought this might be true. Since his policy positions were almost universally conservative, and therefore distinct from those of most Democrats, the conventional wisdom was that Reagan's stance on policy issues simply could not explain his popularity among Democrats.

In 1979, Vince Breglio, my talented colleague, who holds a PhD in psychology, and I conducted an extensive national survey on Reagan's behalf that analyzed the psychological and attitudinal makeup of the American electorate. Once I analyzed the data, it all made perfect sense. I knew Reagan's communication style like the back of my hand. By combining my familiarity of his rhetoric with the study's findings, I was able to solve the mystery of the "Reagan Democrats," even before the term became fashionable.

I'd observed Ronald Reagan's public speeches long enough to know that they typically contained three elements. First, he would begin with a rational component, which he often dovetailed with numbers or factual information. This element was designed to appeal to a voter's sense of logic or reason. Next, Reagan would follow up the rational data with a specific "benefit" or "consequence." This narrowed the universe of possible issue outcomes to exactly two—policy would either help you or hurt you. By placing a rhetorical "fork" in his speeches, Reagan could confront listeners with a singular reality: "We can make one of two choices—the right one or the wrong one. But either way, for good or ill, governmental policies impact your life directly. So choose wisely." Now, up to this point, one might say, "Well, of course. Isn't this the structure all effective persuasion takes?" And the answer is yes, great communicators often adopt this structure. But the Greatest Communicator went one step further, and that's where Reagan's unique use of values comes into play.

What differentiated Reagan from other leaders was his integration of emotion as a third component designed to tap into a person's values. By peeling back the surface layer of a given policy, Reagan would link an issue to a person's most deeply held beliefs. While "policy" connotes that which is mundane and removed from daily life, using *values* triggers policy's antithesis—passion, intimacy, and that which is personally relevant to the individual. Whereas the second component (consequence or benefit) forces a choice between a policy that will either positively or negatively affect a person's self-interest, Reagan's third component (reaching values through emotion) went the extra communicative mile. It showed the audience that the battle being waged transcended Harold Laswell's famous definition of politics as a squabble over "who gets what, when, and how."

No. This, Reagan understood, was about *much* more. It was a battle for our most deeply cherished beliefs and ideals. Communicating this way had the effect of transforming a campaign into a tug-of-war with values as its rope. Thus an election became a collective response to the shared beliefs of the national community.

So when it came time to frame Reagan's speech for the 1980 Republican National Convention in Detroit, I was determined to make sure we preserved the rhetorical design that had served him throughout his political career.

Early on, Reagan made it clear that he wanted his acceptance speech to mark the beginning of his general election campaign and to serve as a unifying force for both the party and the nation. He knew the address would draw the largest audience of his political life. I provided the strategic framework for the speech. One of Reagan's talented wordsmiths, Peter Hannaford, wrote most of the words. The two of us literally locked ourselves in a room to fine-tune the speech until about twenty minutes before Reagan delivered it.

Reagan's acceptance address centered around three value-laden institutions and two values that typified his philosophy. These words were: *family, work, neighborhood, peace,* and *freedom.* By displaying these terms prominently at the beginning of his speech, Reagan drew attention to their importance and previewed the structure of his address:

> I'm very proud of our party tonight. This convention has shown to all America a party united, with positive programs for solving the nation's problems; a party ready to build a new consensus with all those across the land who share a community of values embodied in these words: family, work, neighborhood, peace, and freedom.

For some time, Reagan's focus had been on drawing sharp contrasts between his leadership and Carter's, and to drive home his points he used emotion and value-laden terms designed to tap into deeply held beliefs. For example, in his 1980 acceptance speech, he said, "We face a disintegrating economy," establishing the factual/rational component. Then he laid out the consequence: "Ours are not problems of abstract economic theory. They are problems of flesh and blood." Finally, he brought it all home, motivating through references to emotion: "[These are] problems that cause pain and destroy the moral fiber of real people who should not suffer the further indignity of being told by the government that it is all somehow their fault. We do not have inflation because, as Mr. Carter says, we've lived too well."

In another example, when he asserted, "The American people are carrying the heaviest peacetime tax burden in our nation's history," he again established a factual/rational component, which he followed up with a consequence: "Thanks to the economic policies of the Democratic Party, millions of Americans find themselves out of work." And once again he finished up with an emotional component: "It's time to put America back to work, to make our cities and towns resound with the confident voices of men and women of all races, nationalities, and faiths bringing home to their families a paycheck they can cash for honest money. . . . For those who've abandoned hope, we'll restore hope and we'll welcome them into a great national crusade to make America great again."

These examples show how effective speakers such as Reagan persuade audiences. Reagan understood that mindlessly saying the words "family values" or telling people to "be patriotic," as so many politicians do, accomplishes nothing. You don't *say* you value something. You *show* you do by speaking about it in ways that are personally relevant. Communicators must tap into an audience's emotions if they want to propel people toward action.

Another key component of Reagan's ability to persuade through reason by motivating through emotion, and an incredibly effective means of conveying core values in personally relevant ways, was his integration of stories in his communications. Stories work because they don't raise the red flag of the "hard sell," and indeed, Reagan used them to let the *audience* link the rational to the emotional for themselves. Thus he allowed people to read their own meanings into the message. Yet regardless of what a listener's personal interpretation may have been, Reagan's narratives all redounded to his benefit, because he told stories that were impossible to interpret negatively. And allowing audiences to discover their own meanings had a final advantage: it directly involved the audience and required them to engage the message emotionally, thereby increasing the likelihood that they would retain his message. It was a stroke of rhetorical genius.

And it came naturally for Reagan. He had surrounded himself with a lot of smart people. These were individuals with expensive diplomas on their walls, impressive résumés, and experience working among some of America's sharpest minds. But it was the kid from Dixon, Illinois, who had played football in college, worked in radio, and ended up on the big screen who possessed an intuitive knowledge of communication that far eclipsed anything any of us could offer him.

Sometimes I think he found it amusing. A room full of "experts" standing around all scratching their heads about how to communicate some complex policy—and then the kid from Dixon would say, "Don't worry, fellas. I know just what to say." And he *would* know just what to say. It would always be the right thing to say, and emotion would almost always be at the center of the message.

Many politicians feel uncomfortable infusing emotion into their oratory, but ignoring this element of communication is a mistake, particularly in the age of television. After all, television thrives on its ability to convey emotion. To be sure, speakers can go overboard in their use of emotion by banging the drum of values too forcefully. But having spent most of his life having his face and voice beamed into millions of American homes, Reagan had mastered the medium.

Persuade through reason; motivate through emotion—it was one of the greatest communicative lessons Ronald Reagan ever taught me.

The 1980 Republican Convention taught me other lessons as well. One of them revolved around Reagan's selection of a vice presidential running mate. Since George W. Bush's victory in 2000, historians and presidential scholars have grown increasingly interested in how Ronald Reagan had selected his father, George H. W. Bush, as his running mate. Indeed, the issue raises an interesting question: would George W. Bush have become president had his father not done so before him?

Only a handful of individuals were directly involved in helping Ronald Reagan generate the short list of his potential candidates for vice president. Even fewer participated in the negotiations that took place behind closed doors.

In the world of presidential politics, choosing a running mate remains one of the most important decisions a candidate can make. It's at the top of something I like to call "key action parameters," which is a fancy way of saying "the things a candidate *can* control" in a political environment riddled with unexpected and uncontrollable events. By providing geographical and ideological balance, vice presidential choices can add appeal to a party's ticket. So long before we rolled into Detroit for the Republican national convention, Reagan asked me to study the issue carefully.

In the spring of 1980, I conducted a one-hour-in-home survey exploring voters' opinions and perceptions of roughly twenty potential vice presidential running mates. One of the most important questions we asked was open-ended: "Whom would you like to see Ronald Reagan choose as his running mate?" The data were revealing. Voters had strong preferences toward three men: 20 percent said they wanted George H. W. Bush; 14 percent named Senator Howard Baker; and 13 percent cited former president Gerald Ford. By the middle of June, I had analyzed these findings alongside a host of other questions and was ready to present my results. Keeping the media in suspense, however, was critical. With the ego and future support of the vice presidential contenders hanging in the balance, we were extremely cautious about keeping our results close to the vest. Ronald Reagan, Bill Casey, and Ed Meese were the only individuals I briefed.

Although Bush rated highest, there were other factors to consider. One of these involved Bush calling Reagan's economic policy "voodoo economics." Not surprisingly, the comment had angered Reagan. Still, my polling data had confirmed that Bush had a lot to offer. His background as head of the CIA meant he was a man who could be trusted. And on a personal level, I always found him to be a gentleman. But I wasn't the one running for president.

Reagan felt Bush had violated the "eleventh commandment," something the governor believed in deeply. The eleventh commandment: never attack a fellow Republican in the primary.

But there was another reason the candidate wasn't ready to commit—he liked to keep his options open. To Reagan, having a broad range of options from which to choose was almost always the best policy. So we employed the services of a well-known New York lawyer and alumnus of the Treasury Department, Edward Schmults, to thoroughly vet a dozen or so of the top-tier vice presidential candidates. As Ed Meese explained in an article in the *Hoover Digest*:

> Following Schmults's work, these extensive and multifaceted preparations were closely held among five individuals—Casey, Wirthlin, the candidate and his wife, and me—and no word that they even existed leaked to the press, the public, or a wider circle of others heavily involved in the campaign.

Thus, despite the fact that my vice presidential findings had been completed in time to be included in the Black Book, no mention was made of a vice presidential selection strategy.

Reagan needed a running mate who could appeal to the moderate elements of the party without alienating those conservatives who remained the governor's bedrock of support. Stu Spencer, one of Reagan's longtime advisers and a mentor of mine, instilled in me an axiom that has always guided my philosophy of political strategy, and that is that a candidate should always go to his core support first. He must first deal to strength. Once his base has been galvanized, a candidate can then go after the undecided voter.

Choosing Ford would have sent a strong signal to moderate voters. That Ford had already served as president would also add considerable stature to the ticket. On paper, it looked like a reasonable plan. While the 1976 campaign had produced some bad blood between Reagan and Ford, time had healed most of those wounds. Reagan's battle scars administered at the hands of Bush, however, were still fresh. The governor made it known that the sting from Bush's words had not yet faded. So, with a Bush selection seemingly off the table, Casey and Meese agreed I should discuss the Ford option with Reagan.

During my conversation with the candidate, I highlighted five of Ford's strengths. First, he brought something right out of the box, which was near-universal name recognition. Second, he had the ability to appeal to a different group of voters. Third, Ford did not require any start-up time and could start campaigning immediately. Fourth, the announcement would be dramatic and therefore likely to garner positive media attention. Finally, given that we anticipated a close election, Ford just might be the difference between winning and losing. Toward the end of the conversation, I framed the issue for Reagan in personal terms.

"Governor, suppose that in 1976, in spite of the signals that were sent to the Ford people that you didn't want to be vice president, President Ford came to you in a private way and said, 'Governor, I need you. The country needs you. Your being on the ticket can make the difference between my beating Jimmy Carter and my losing him.' Governor, what would you have done if that kind of appeal had been made in that way?"

"Dick, I would have accepted," Reagan replied.

"Governor, can you afford not to give Gerald Ford the same opportunity?" I asked.

"No," said Reagan.

So the decision was made to reach out to Ford. Over three days' time, Casey, Meese, and I entered into a series of private meetings with Ford's team, which consisted of Robert Barrett, Alan Greenspan, Henry Kissinger, and Jack Marsh. With us we brought ten talking points that had been crafted in conjunction with Reagan. While the deliberations remained cordial throughout, the longer we discussed what a Reagan-Ford administration might look like, the more clear it became that Ford's team was on a different wavelength. The Ford team's overall tone led us to believe that Ford would not be content playing the traditional role of simply a vice president. Still, as was Reagan's style, we were careful to explore all options without committing the governor to anything.

The Reagan-Ford alliance had already begun to look less and less likely. But if anyone had any doubts, they were shattered in Reagan's convention suite at the Detroit Plaza Hotel. Reagan, Marty Anderson, Dick Allen, Lyn Nofziger, myself, and others were all sitting in front of the room's three television sets. Those were the good old days before twenty-four-hour cable news when there were only three major networks. The TV tuned to CBS grabbed our attention. Unbeknownst to us, Walter Cronkite had scheduled an interview with Gerald Ford. When Ford appeared onscreen, the room fell silent. The press had apparently gotten wind of our deliberations with him. And that's when Cronkite put the issue to Ford squarely. He asked the former president whether a Reagan-Ford administration would necessarily resemble a "co-presidency."

The phrase shot out of the reporter's mouth like a verbal arrow aimed at Ronald Reagan. When Ford failed to correct Cronkite or downplay the idea, Reagan catapulted off the couch.

"Did you hear what he just said about a co-presidency?!" Reagan howled. He was shocked. It wasn't an angry response. It was more of a sense of genuine surprise, because we had tried to keep the whole issue under wraps.

I remember thinking: *Well, that's the end of that.*

And it was.

But in the interim we were going to have to do some serious damage control. And quickly! The Cronkite interview had triggered a ticking time bomb. Casey, Meese, and I knew it was critical we quash the suggestion of a Reagan-Ford alliance. Allowing a rumor like that to spread would only raise some delegates' expectations of a Reagan-Ford pairing, a tandem some were calling the "dream ticket."

Casey, Meese, and I must have looked like the Keystone Cops. Piling into cars, scurrying around the convention center, and hustling in and out of hotel rooms, we were determined to douse the Ford fire before it spread. But from the time Reagan asked me to study the vice presidential issue the campaign's plan had remained unchanged: maximize the governor's chances of victory by selecting a running mate who would appeal to more moderate elements of the party. As it turned out, Ford made the situation much easier when he graciously withdrew his name from consideration. Reagan considered it a class act.

With the Ford option off the table, I threw my support behind my original choice, George H. W. Bush. I had a powerful card to play—data. Reagan had to make his decision quickly. And he did. When he telephoned to extend the offer, he asked Bush whether he could fully support the party platform. Bush assured him that he could, and the deal was made.

In the end, I believe we got the best of both worlds. Reagan got the more centrist Republican he needed without having to give up decision-making authority. Still, while Bush complemented Reagan, both would have admitted that they were completely different types of men. Reagan was the natural. Bush was textbook. What's more, the men saw themselves in different ways. Their egos and levels of inner confidence had sprung from different wells.

One story that illustrates this happened during the 1980 convention in Detroit. After Reagan tapped Bush as his running mate, a group of us enjoyed breakfast together while visiting in Reagan's hotel suite. The suite had a common room for hosting guests that was sandwiched between two bedrooms on each side. Bush, Reagan, myself, and some others had been chatting with a mayor from a key battleground state. Wanting to ingratiate himself to the newly nominated presidential candidate, the mayor said, "My, Governor, you sure look great for a man your age in the midst of political battle. How do you manage to stay in such great physical shape?"

Without saying a word, Reagan got up out of his seat and

disappeared into his bedroom. When he returned, in his hand was an exercise wheel. The thing sort of looked like a doughnut with a stick running through its middle. "Here's my secret, Mr. Mayor," said Reagan. And with that, the former Eureka College football player, still wearing his suit, dropped to his knees and placed one hand on each of the bars protruding from the wheel. In one long, graceful motion, Reagan stretched his body forward, distributing his weight from his knees to his hands, until his chest hovered inches above the floor. With equal fluidity, he then pulled back on the wheel, recoiling his body like a Slinky before returning to his original position.

"Wow," said the mayor. "I guess doing that every day *would* keep a man pretty fit."

After we had finished visiting, everyone left the hotel room, or so I thought. Savoring the rare moment of tranquillity, I sat down on one of the low-slung couches in the now darkened visiting room and sat silently thinking through what the day might bring. That's when I noticed that someone else was in the room. It was Bush. He walked over to Reagan's little exercise wheel. Curiosity, it seems, had gotten the best of this former Yale University baseball player.

Sitting perfectly motionless, I thought to myself: *I've got to see this.*

Mimicking Reagan's earlier demonstration, Bush dropped down onto his knees. Steadying himself, he put one hand on each side of the wheel and began to lean forward. But as the wheel rolled out about two and a half feet, he began to lose his balance. With shaking hands and wobbling shoulders, his elbows gave way, sending him crashing face forward onto the carpet.

I rustled my papers to let him know someone was in the room. Startled, Bush wrenched his neck around. When our eyes met, he realized for the first time that he was not alone. He popped up off the ground, and blew by me on his way out the door without saying a word. It was one of the most unforgettable things I'd ever experienced.

Reagan's hotel suite in Detroit was also the site of another special memory that brought insight into Reagan's character. After winning the nomination, Nancy and the governor had invited a small group of us back to their suite to celebrate. My wife, Jeralie, and I had been chatting with friends when the governor motioned to us from across the room. Once we made contact, Reagan ushered us into his private bedroom.

"I wanted to tell you how much I appreciate your efforts in making tonight possible," he said.

"Well, Governor, it is truly an honor. I've got to think that you must be exhausted. The campaign and the convention have been a whirlwind. I bet this has been quite a drain on you," I said.

"Well, not really, Dick. I guess it sort of reminds me of a story I heard recently about a man who passed away and dreamed he was walking on the beach with the Lord. As he looked behind him he saw that his footprints in the sand had traced out his life's course. He noticed that at his lowest and darkest point there was only one pair of footprints in the sand. So he asked God, 'Why in my greatest times of need did you desert me, Father?' The Lord replied, 'When you saw only one pair of footprints I didn't desert you. I carried you.' That's how I feel. I felt Him carrying me, Dick."

You might recognize Reagan's story as the now famous poem "Footprints in the Sand." That was the first time my wife and I had heard the poem recited, and from the mouth of the master storyteller no less. It was a window into Ronald Reagan. His depth of faith and solemn belief in the power of a loving God were not part of some obligatory political nod to religiosity. It was real. I never saw Ronald Reagan wear his spirituality on his sleeve, but neither was it something he kept hidden away. I don't think he could have if he tried. His faith was woven into the fabric of his being, and it affected the way he lived and saw the world. Leaving his belief in God at the door would not only have been disingenuous, it would have been hypocritical. I can honestly say Reagan's faith guided many of the decisions he made as well as the way he treated people. In a word, his relationship with the Almighty was "genuine."

Yet as I found out after the convention in Detroit, Reagan's spiritual depth and generous spirit were matched by only one thing: his stubbornness. At the outset of his 1980 general election campaign, I learned the hard way just *how* stubborn he could be when I tried to get between him and his previous commitment to speak to an audience. Indeed, my battle with Reagan over his scheduled speech at the Neshoba County Fair in Philadelphia, Mississippi, produced one of the most awkward moments of our relationship.

Having just been selected the Republican candidate for president, Reagan needed to break out of the California mold. In order to communicate his concern over the plight of African Americans who had been abandoned by the failed policies of an inefficient and uncompassionate welfare state, the campaign had planned a major trip to inner-city New York to communicate, one-on-one, with the citizens most affected by Carter's policies. The trouble was that a group of Mississippi Republicans had convinced Reagan to deliver a speech at the Neshoba County Fair only days before his major campaign kickoff in New York.

Others and I had planned for the New York venue to be the opening move of the 1980 campaign. The event had been designed to illustrate the present and future consequences of a welfare system that had trapped citizens in a cruel cycle of dependency and to communicate the governor's compassion for those who had borne government's burdens most harshly. In other words, the New York event was everything the Neshoba venue wasn't. New York was urban and more likely to establish a candidate's legitimacy on the national stage. Neshoba was rural and therefore more locally focused. The New York setting was all about the future. The Neshoba venue was for some a reflection of a gruesome racist event of the past. Let me explain.

As Reagan's strategist, one of my primary duties involved making certain the candidate never found himself in settings where he could be easily misrepresented by media. For a man who spent his life in front of a camera, Reagan was sometimes surprisingly naïve about some reporters' desire to sever content from context by grafting their own views onto a story. This blind spot meant I had to be alert. I've always believed the best strategy for putting out a fire is to never let one start in the first place. I tried to make sure every speaking venue we scheduled reinforced Ronald Reagan's ethos and left little room for mis-interpretation or, worse, manipulation. So when I found out that someone had convinced my candidate to deliver a speech at the Neshoba County Fair in Philadelphia, Mississippi, I immediately saw the dark clouds of political miscalculation gathering on the not-so-distant horizon.

In 1964, three civil rights advocates—James Chaney, Andrew Goodman, and Michael Schwerner—had been mur-dered in cold blood in Neshoba County. Their crime? Helping African Americans register to vote. Later, in 1966, invoking the names of these men whose lives hatred had claimed, Dr. Martin Luther King Jr. returned to Neshoba County to recount the tragic story of their slaying. Philadelphia, Mississippi, therefore, was rightly imbued with important his-toric and symbolic meaning. By 1980, while time had healed some of the wounds, racism's scars still remained. But that only begins to explain Reagan's desire to speak at this place. The rest of the story had occurred decades ago in Dixon, Illinois, the site of Reagan's childhood.

Reagan said he grew up in a family where there was no sin worse than racial bigotry. Upon the release of the movie *The*

Birth of a Nation, Ronald Reagan's father forbade him and his brother from seeing it because he didn't like that it contained favorable depictions of the Ku Klux Klan. Lessons such as these produced a man who was truly color-blind. Frankly, I don't believe Reagan ever fully understood the multilayered nuances of the "image politics" that surround race in America. His view was that racism was evil, period. Because as the son of an Irish Catholic shoe salesman he had been on the receiving end of discrimination himself, it's easy to understand why he had no tolerance for bigots. As his friend and fellow Eureka College lineman William Franklin Burghardt put it, "I just don't think he was conscious of race at all." And of all people, Burghardt was certainly in a position to know.

The Eureka College football team had been scheduled to play an away game in Reagan's hometown of Dixon, Illinois. Unbeknownst to Burghardt and another African American player, their presence had prompted a hotel owner to deny them lodging. After the coach threatened to take the team's business elsewhere, he had been met with a sad (if factual) retort from the hotel owner: "No hotel in Dixon is going to take colored boys." Not wanting his black teammates to feel uncomfortable, or to be hurt by the hotel owner's racist attitude, a young Ronald Reagan devised a plan. He advised the coach to tell the two black players that there wasn't enough room in the hotel and that they would have to break up the team for the night. Then, Reagan counseled, he and his two black teammates could take a cab and stay at his parents' house.

And that's exactly what they did. That night the future president's mother, Nelle Reagan, answered her doorbell and welcomed the three young men into her home. True to the lessons she had instilled in her children, she too was color-blind. Sadly, in politics this is not always the case. While Ronald Reagan might not have seen any problems with speaking in Neshoba County, I knew others might.

This Neshoba appearance is going to be a disaster, I thought.

I knew television channels would replay clips of the Neshoba event alongside negative Democratic commentary. In other words, Reagan was about to dive into electoral quicksand, and I felt like I had to do something. So I sped over to his home in the hopes of changing his mind before he left California. When I arrived, he was in the master bedroom standing at the foot of the bed. He was holding a stack of papers about fifty or so pages thick, the contents of his Neshoba speech among them. *Just in time!* I thought.

"Hey, Dick, just looking over the speech. How are you doing?" he asked.

Sitting down on the edge of the governor's bed, I began to plead my case.

"Not good, Governor. I'm concerned we're about to make a huge mistake. I'm deeply troubled by your decision to speak at the Neshoba County Fair in Mississippi. Governor, this is a major miscalculation on your part. I understand you've made a commitment to speak to friends of yours in Mississippi, many of whom have supported you for some time. But this all stands to negate our positive outreach in New York. The media and the Democrats are going to have a field day with this. Every election has its turning points. This could be the foothold your opponents need. I don't think you understand how they will play this. You can't give this speech."

Both pollsters and strategists have the unenviable task of sometimes telling candidates things they don't want to hear. In my career I've had a double dose, because I've often worn both hats. But despite my experience being the bearer of bad news, this time I was committing some major blunders.

My first mistake was telling Ronald Reagan he couldn't do something, a grievous error to be sure. There was sometimes a direct correlation between how hard you pushed and how deeply he dug in his heels. My second mistake involved ignoring the cautionary nonverbal signals his body sent screaming my way. Having worked with Reagan for eleven years up to this point, I knew his body language well. All signs pointed to "STOP." But meeting stubbornness with stubbornness, I pressed on.

"You simply *cannot* give this speech," I implored.

"Dick, one thing I learned as an actor was that once the billing is set you don't pull out. Now, don't tell me what I can and can't do. *I'm* the one running for president. I'm giving this speech, and I'm giving it at the Neshoba County Fair!" he exclaimed.

"Governor, as your friend, I can tell you that despite your best intentions, and despite what you may think about the importance of keeping your word to your supporters in Neshoba, the media is going to make you out to be an insensitive raci——"

He'd heard enough.

"I'M GIVING THIS SPEECH!" he barked.

At this, he swung back his arm, stared me in the eyes, and hurled all thirty-plus pages of his speech into the air, leaving me sitting on his bed in a blizzard of cascading papers.

There are awkward moments, and then there are awkward *moments. This was one of the latter.*

I froze.

He froze.

I didn't really know what to do. Honestly, I don't think he did either. We just sort of stared at each other, expressionless, as if to say, "Okay, now what just happened here, exactly?"

To this day I don't remember who picked up the pages of that speech. But the experience taught me two things. First, his show of temper, although rare, could be explosive. And second, Ronald Reagan believed that his personal commitment to people and his message were worth fighting for. And that's the point. He was willing to endure the political costs our opponents' spin might exact in order to make good on his word.

But at that moment, sitting in his bedroom, I had been the obstacle separating him from the people he wanted to spend time with. In his mind, that was unacceptable. Supporters had invited him to speak, and he wanted the chance to connect with the better virtues of the Neshoba audience. Hearing someone close to him bring up the R word—"racist"—had been the last straw. As Reagan confessed in his autobiography, *An American Life*: "Whatever the reasons for the myth that I'm a racist, I blow my top every time I hear it."

I can certainly vouch for that!

As for the fallout from his speech, sadly, my instincts proved correct. The *Washington Post* ran an August 11 editorial with the incendiary headline: "Chilling Words in Neshoba County— Is Reagan Saying That He Intends to Do Everything He Can to Turn the Clock Back to the Mississippi Justice of 1964?" Others piled on as well. But Reagan was willing to endure the unfair smears and name-calling. He knew it was nothing more than a cynical campaign ploy designed to divide rather than unite. Indeed, one of the reasons he was able to use words so masterfully to galvanize public opinion was that he refused to kowtow to the elite and often shrill voices of those who spent their lives carping comfortably from the sidelines of leadership.

And for good reason. Audiences like to feel connected to speakers. People don't like "speeches," they like conversations. Listeners want to believe a leader is speaking directly to them and no one else. This means leaders must collapse the communicative distance between them and their audience. And that's why Reagan loved to be close to people, literally. For example, every time we set up a speaking event he would have us instruct the advance man to make sure the podium was no more than eight feet from the audience. Also, when possible, the house lights were to be turned up. Like a canoeist reading the shifting currents of a river, Reagan liked to read the non-verbal responses of his audience so he could adjust his message as he spoke. For some, his methods may have initially appeared unorthodox. But effective leadership demands deviation.

Throughout the 1980 general election against President

Jimmy Carter, the governor focused on drawing a sharp contrast between his brand of optimistic leadership and the incumbent president's "malaise"-filled messages. Indeed, two major communicative hurdles stood between Reagan and winning the White House. The first of these was something called the "October Surprise."

When devising political strategy, I always start by studying my opponent. I want to know him better than he knows himself, and the 1980 presidential election was no different. Before I wrote the Black Book, I went to school on Jimmy Carter and his strategist, Patrick H. Caddell.

Caddell had made my efforts much easier when, following Carter's 1976 victory, somehow his findings from his campaign memoranda and strategies were made available to the media. These documents allowed us to study his moves, his fundamental base of set assumptions, and how he thought. And as for Carter, the more I learned the more convinced I became that he was considerably tougher than his public persona suggested. These were two men who played for keeps.

Still, not in a million years did we think Jimmy Carter would *himself* play the role of attack dog. Yet that is exactly what happened. He came out swinging. His campaign accused Reagan of being a warmongering cowboy with little concern for the less fortunate. Instead of having only his surrogates launch the attacks, Carter was doing some of it himself. Honestly, it surprised us. The decision to put Carter on the offensive stood in contradistinction to his image as a genial "man of the people."

One of the other things I decided to study was which of Carter's actions or attacks voters would find most salient. The data were alarming. While Governor Reagan appeared well positioned for victory, one issue in particular could give Carter as much as a ten-point bump. Worse still, the issue was entirely beyond our control.

Were President Carter to negotiate the release of the fifty-two American hostages being held in Tehran, my studies suggested voters might be primed to reward him with reelection. To verify my initial soundings, I conducted a historical study, "The Impact of Crises on the Presidential Vote." Against this historical "baseline" we ran ongoing research. Moreover, we knew that some in the Carter camp weren't above manipulating political events to benefit his electoral prospects.

Carter had a reputation for timing events with elections. For example, after he suffered two major losses in New York and Connecticut during the Democratic primaries, heading into the Wisconsin Democratic presidential primary, Carter staged a press conference wherein he announced a "positive step" forward in the U.S. efforts to free the hostages. Later it was revealed by a Carter insider that there had been no positive step whatsoever.

What's more, further into the campaign we were getting word, back channel, that hospital beds were being prepared in Wiesbaden, Germany, and that recovery planes were being readied at Andrews Air Force Base.

When I alerted Casey and Meese about the electoral consequences of a cynically timed hostage release, all agreed it was essential that we monitor the situation closely. Since several of us had places at the Skyline Apartments in Falls Church, Virginia, we decided to discuss the situation each morning.

During those meetings I advised that since there wasn't much we could do directly if the hostages came home, our best bet was to inoculate voters on the issue by conditioning them to expect that Carter might try to spring an "October Surprise" just before the election. (A former employee of mine and a talented strategic thinker, Gary Lawrence, had coined the phrase "October Surprise" during a strategy session.) I considered the issue pivotal. Thus, I included a discussion of what the Reagan campaign's strategy should be in the Black Book, which was completed in June 1980. In that discussion I outlined a three-part strategy for key campaign personnel to follow: they should begin to sprinkle their conversation with references to Carter's October Surprise; they should precondition the American people to see Carter's October maneuverings in a more cynical perspective; and they should simply raise the question, without volunteering their own ideas, to spur people to their own imaginings on what the surprise might be.

We needed to build all the contingencies we could possibly conjure up in order to prepare ourselves to change the nature, thrust, and scope of the campaign, dramatically if necessary, right up to election day. My data led me to believe that in order for Carter to be effective, the release would have to happen sometime between October 18 and 25. Beyond October 25 voters would meet a potential hostage release with increasing political cynicism.

We weren't going to take any chances. So we set aside roughly $200,000 for possible radio and television ads. In fact, we had already prepared tapes in the event they were needed. They never were.

As for Reagan, he generally felt we were as prepared as we could be. Whenever we would talk about Carter, he displayed the same kind of respect a boxer shows another boxer. He recognized his opponent's talents and trained accordingly, all the while knowing that Carter the pugilist fully intended to knock him out. Sadly, Carter wasn't above resorting at times to hitting below the belt. While speaking to a largely African American church audience, Carter said, "You've seen in this campaign the stirrings of hate and the rebirth of code words like 'states' rights' in a speech in Missisissippi [a reference to Reagan's Neshoba County Fair speech]; in a campaign reference to the Ku Klux Klan relating to the South. This is a message that creates a cloud on the political horizon. Hatred has no place in this country."

It was a sad example of attack-style politics.

When the final bell rang, the two men would shake hands and walk away from the battle. In the meantime, we followed the prescriptions outlined in the Black Book in order to buffer against an October Surprise. Of course, Carter was never able to broker a deal to have our American hostages returned.

On the day of Reagan's inauguration, however, the hostages were freed. The timing of the release gave some Democrats reason to grouse that William Casey and George Bush, both former CIA men, had somehow thwarted the release of the hostages until after the election. A few years after Reagan's second term, the Democrats even went so far as to churn the conspiracy theories into a full-blown $4.5 million investigation in the House of Representatives. When the final report was published, it stated that there was no credible evidence of any wrongdoing. Ironically enough, the findings seemed to indicate that it was Carter, not Reagan, who might have tried to use the hostage crisis to influence primary voters.

Personally, I have always felt that the timing of the release had more to do with the Iranians wanting to stick it to Jimmy Carter than anything else. But either way, after the hostages had been held captive for 444 days, the one thing Jimmy Carter and Ronald Reagan could agree on was that their release was a moment for celebration.

The October Surprise was the equivalent of a submerged electoral iceberg, one that held the ability to wreck Ronald Reagan's chances at victory. But having circumnavigated that obstacle, Reagan would face a second test—debating Jimmy Carter—that would require him to use his entire rhetorical arsenal.

Ever since John F. Kennedy and Richard Nixon squared off in the first televised presidential debate in 1960, the verbal sparring sessions between presidential candidates have produced some of the most exciting communicative events of presidential elections. The reason for this is simple. No matter how hard candidates prepare, debates are inherently unpredictable. More than that, for the candidate leading in the polls, they can be risky. Like the time Gerald Ford seemed to forget where Poland was located. Or the time Lloyd Bentsen turned to a young Dan Quayle and boomed, "You're no Jack Kennedy." Or when Al Gore sighed endlessly into his microphone when facing off with then governor George W. Bush.

Indeed, debates are more likely to be remembered for the "moments" they produce than the substance candidates discuss. Once these moments bounce through the media echo chamber, trouble can arise. The last thing you want is for your candidate to become fodder for a *Saturday Night Live* skit or one of David Letterman's or Jay Leno's punch lines. While being the butt of a national joke might seem insignificant, studies have shown that these sources of information can influence some voters' perceptions of political figures.

As a voter, I love the high-stakes nature of presidential debates. Having said that, I have a confession to make: I didn't want Ronald Reagan to debate Jimmy Carter. Indeed, as a strategist, I've always approached debates with caution. The reason wasn't that I lacked confidence in Reagan, it was that I had supreme confidence that Reagan was going to win *regardless* of whether he debated Jimmy Carter or not.

But the fighter in him saw it differently. Reagan believed that if he was to assume his opponent's title he should be willing to go toe to toe with him in a presidential debate. And so during a private meeting held in the Waldorf Astoria, Reagan told us he had decided he would debate Jimmy Carter in a single debate to be held one week before voters headed to the polls.

Honestly, I think he relished the chance to debate Carter live before an audience of millions. He had been speaking to audiences all his life, and the Irishman in him loved a good confrontation. As soon as he made his decision, Reagan dropped into debate preparation mode. His days in Hollywood had taught him the importance of research and rehearsal. And so the candidate and a core group of us began prepping him for the debate.

In addition to compiling a series of debate prep books, the campaign decided to rent a space where we could hold mock debates. The role of Jimmy Carter was to be played by Congressman David Stockman, the man who would later become Reagan's budget director. The mock debates themselves were held at Wexford House, the former home of Elizabeth Taylor and her now ex-husband United States senator John Warner. The site was warm, yet professional. Reagan would come in wearing a T-shirt, and the tone before each session was light. But during the first confrontation between Stockman and Reagan, that sentiment quickly changed.

As was his style, Stockman went after Reagan full throttle. He cited statistics, questioned the governor's record, and undermined his arguments every chance he got. At one point, I remember the governor became so annoyed with Stockman/Carter that he showed a flash of anger and exasperation. But that first session was important, because it reminded Reagan of just how tenacious Carter would be.

With each subsequent round, Reagan improved. One of the last areas to be polished was his closing statement to the television viewers. Each candidate's closing statement would be the last thing viewers heard. It needed to summarize the reasons for electing Reagan in convincing fashion.

James Baker suggested that David Gergen and I might want to craft some brief remarks for Reagan to use in his closing statement. Gergen is a talented wordsmith, and the synergy between us helped produce one of Reagan's most devastating lines in the 1980 debate.

I told Gergen that one of Reagan's most impressive communicative tools was his use of rhetorical questions. Ever since we started out in 1968, I had seen him use this technique to great effect out on the stump. So we began brainstorming what question Reagan might ask voters. I said that one of the most common questions pollsters ask is something called the "wrong track/right track" question: "In your opinion, is the country on the right track or the wrong track?" I had been asking it for years, and the media often rely on this statistic to get a sense of the country's mood, to sense voters' appetite for change. From there, we began crafting a string of rhetorical questions—the answers to which we knew would resoundingly favor our candidate—designed to convince voters that it was time for new leadership. Here is a portion of what Reagan said in his closing statement:

> Next Tuesday all of you will go to the polls, will stand there in the polling place and make a decision. I think when you make that decision, it might be well if you would ask yourself: Are you better off than you were four years ago? Is it easier for you to go and buy things in the stores than it was four years ago? Is there more or less unemployment in the country than there was four years ago? Is America as respected throughout the world as it was? Do you feel that our security is as safe, that we're as strong as we were four years ago? And if you answer all of those questions yes, why then, I think your choice is very obvious as to whom you will vote for. If you don't agree, if you don't think that this course that we've been on for the last four years is what you would like to see us follow for the next four, then I could suggest another choice that you have.

Even as I type those lines I can still hear Ronald Reagan's voice saying them. I can still picture him looking into the camera and making you feel the weight of his words. While Gergen and I helped craft the lines, it was Reagan's use of rhetorical questions combined with his unrivaled ability to breathe life into a text that made his closing statement the knockout punch it became. Nancy described it best in her autobiography, *My Turn*, when she wrote, "It was Ronnie's final statement in the debate that really sealed Jimmy Carter's fate.

This was vintage Ronnie—clear, personal, and empathetic."

The other big help in the Reagan/Carter debate came from Jimmy Carter himself. He helped us in two ways. First, his outlandish charges gave Reagan the chance to drop his now famous brush-off line. With a tilt of the head and a smile, Reagan just said, "There you go again." It was an enormously effective way to defuse Carter's attacks without appearing defensive.

Carter's second gift came when he oddly inserted his daughter, Amy, into the debate. In reference to a question about nuclear proliferation, here's how President Carter answered:

"I had a discussion with my daughter, Amy, the other day, before I came here, to ask her what the most important issue was. She said she thought nuclear weaponry—and the control of nuclear arms."

What made this an odd response? Amy Carter was only twelve years old.

Our polling showed that the all-important independent voters had by almost a two-to-one margin declared Ronald Reagan the winner of the first and only debate of the 1980 election. While many political scientists contend that debates seldom change voters' minds, many agree they galvanize preexisting opinions. If that is true, the governor's debate performance solidified what the majority of America already knew: Ronald Reagan was the man who could restore America's confidence in herself and her standing in the world.

Just before election day, I asked two members of my team, Vince Breglio and Richard Beal, to set PINS to the most negative scenarios possible to see what would happen. As they ran dozens of simulations, not a single scenario supported a Carter victory. Hard as they tried, they couldn't find a way for Reagan to lose the election.

Breglio and Beal were anxious to tell me the good news. But I was traveling with the candidate, and there was no one with them at the Century Plaza Hotel in California. So, looking around their paper-filled room, they decided to call for maid service. When the two female maids arrived, Vince and Richard figured, "What the heck." The two men raced up to the maids and shouted, "It's going to be a landslide! It's going to be a landslide!" The women looked at one another quizzically and then back at Vince and Richard.

"No habla Ingles," one of them replied.

They must have thought Breglio and Beal were nuts. But whether they are aware of it or not, those two women were the first people in American history to know with a high degree of certainty that Ronald Reagan would win the White House the following day.

Meanwhile, while Beal and Breglio had spent their day with PINS, I was on the campaign plane with Nancy and the governor. On Monday, November 3, 1980, we covered a lot of territory. We made five major stops in three states—Illinois, Oregon, and California—closing, of course, in the governor's home state. The last stop was one we had all been looking forward to for more than two years—a rally in San Diego. We couldn't have dreamed of a better finale. Roughly 30,000 people jammed a shopping center parking lot to give a last rousing hurrah to candidate Ronald Reagan.

Despite those successes, however, the day had not been a good one for Nancy Reagan. She had appeared in San Francisco to do a solo venue where she had an encounter with some extremists who had hurled obscene epithets at her and her "Ronnie." When she rejoined us in San Diego and returned to the plane, I could tell she was clearly fatigued. In the front cabin, the crew had surprised us with champagne and a large bowl of iced shrimp. It was a fitting and pleasant culmination to the campaign.

After the governor raised his glass and gave a toast, Nancy turned to me with eyes brimming with hope and anxiety.

"Dick, are we *really* going to win tomorrow?"

"Yes, Nancy, we really are going to win,"

My confidence wasn't based on wishful thinking. The signs of a victory had been clearly evident since mid-October. I had felt the rumblings of a landslide on the previous Friday, the date of our last strategy meeting. My tracking numbers had Reagan with 45 percent of the vote, Jimmy Carter with 36 percent, John Anderson with 8 percent, and 10 percent of the electorate still undecided.

But PINS had given me even greater confidence. Unlike the political pundits and the public, we had never been preoccupied with our overall national standing. Right from the beginning our campaign goal had been to secure a minimum of 270 electors. At earlier campaign strategy meetings I would give an average estimate of the number of electors we could expect to win at that time. These would include optimistic and pessimistic estimates. Two days before the election, a group of top political media personalities and analysts had gathered at the Palm restaurant in Washington, D.C., to offer their predictions for how the election would conclude. They each took a piece of paper and wrote the name of the candidate they thought would win the election. The count: fourteen votes for Carter, one vote too close to call. Not one panelist believed Reagan would win. When I heard about it, I just smiled.

November 4, 1980, was going to be Reagan's day. When I woke up that morning, I looked at myself in the mirror. My hair was as long as it had ever been. The campaign had been so hectic that I hadn't had a haircut in over three months. My locks had grown so long, in fact, that the Secret Service once thought I might be a hippie protestor when I got into a car in the governor's caravan.

Since we had done all we could to position the governor for victory, I decided to pay my barber a long-overdue visit. About halfway through my cut, the barbershop's phone rang. A *New York Times* reporter had tracked me down at about 9 a.m. How he found me at the barbershop, of all places, I haven't the slightest clue. He said the exit polls were all trending our way. "Dick," he said, "it looks like a landslide." With this nugget of information confirming our findings from PINS, I asked my barber if I he wouldn't mind if I placed a call before finishing my haircut. He said that would be fine.

Nancy picked up the phone.

"Is the governor available, Nancy?"

"Dick, I'm afraid he's in the shower right now. Is everything okay?"

"Everything is great. But I really need to speak with him. Could you please get him out of the shower?"

"He's all soapy and wet, Dick."

"I understand. But trust me, it's worth it."

"Hold on."

When Reagan finally came to the phone, I said the words I had been waiting to say ever since our first run in 1976.

"Governor, how would you like to change your title?" I said.

"What do you mean?" he asked.

"Your new title is not going to be governor. Your new title is going to be president," I said.

Silence.

"Governor, are you still there?" I asked.

"I'm here. Well, uh, let's not get ahead of ourselves here. The voting hasn't ended just yet. Let's wait until all the votes are counted before we begin celebrating," he cautioned.

"Well, whatever you want to do is fine with me. But I just wanted you to be the first one to know that you will win today, Mr. President!"

When the votes were tallied, Reagan had won in a landslide, taking forty-four states to Carter's six. In the popular vote, Reagan captured 51 percent, Carter 41 percent, and John Anderson 7 percent. Most importantly, Reagan dominated the field in electoral votes, taking 489 electoral votes to Jimmy Carter's 49.

But as soon as Ronald Reagan began celebrating his landslide victory, the weight of the presidency began descending upon him. While his first term in office would produce unprecedented success, it would also bring him within inches of his life. Indeed, this experience, perhaps more than any other, would refocus Ronald Reagan's sense of purpose for both himself and his presidency.

The 1976 presidential campaign team prior to the New Hampshire primary. Left to right: Lyn Nofziger, me, Peter Hannaford, Martin Anderson, Michael Deaver, Ronald Reagan, and John Sears (seated).

Dear Dick – It was a pleasure having you on our "airline". Very Best Regards. Sincerely Ron

The last hurrah on Air Force One just before election day, November 5, 1988.

…howing the president "Brown's Medfly Swatter."

…ancy Reagan asks: "Dick, are we *really* going to win?" "Yes, Nancy, we …ally are going to win."

Sharing a laugh with the last chief of staff, Ken Duberstein, and the president in the Oval Office, November 3, 1988. The final stretch of our twenty-year run together with just one month left before vacating the Oval Office.

Dear Dick – Even when the news isn't good we like to see you.
Warmest Regards Ron

And the news in that meeting was not all bad—a 69 percent approval rating for the president.

One of my last briefings in the Oval Office with Don Regan and President Reagan.

A pleasant moment shared with the president in the Oval Office.

A monthly briefing: "By a two-to-one ratio, Americans believe President Reagan's proposed tax changes will help the economy."

While challenges loomed on the horizon, Ronald Reagan's presidency was given
76 percent approval rating.

President Reagan visits the Reagan/Bush campaign headquarters, October 1984. That day he shook hands with a hundred of his political foot soldiers.

The news: Americans offer a strong, positive response to the president's speech to the nation, December 1987.

4

"Do You Know What I *Really* Want to Be Remembered For?"

The White House, 1980–1984

We cannot escape our destiny, nor should we try to do so. The leadership of the free world was thrust upon us two centuries ago in that little hall of Philadelphia. . . . We are indeed, and we are today, the last best hope of man on earth.

—Ronald Reagan, "A City on a Hill," First Conservative
Political Action Conference, January 25, 1974

The sounds of shuffling feet and chattering celebrants could be heard through the slender curtain separating us from the Reagan faithful who had assembled in the ballroom of the Century Plaza Hotel in Los Angeles. They had gathered to celebrate Ronald Reagan's victory and to welcome the newly elected president back home, if only briefly, before he and Nancy would swap coasts as their permanent place of residence.

Behind the curtain, however, an entirely different scene was unfolding.

Before taking the stage, Reagan and I had been discussing how perfectly the events of the last three weeks had all turned out. His landslide win had been the result of years of planning and hard work. With the climax now behind us, we were all looking forward to a restful denouement. After months of campaigning, it was finally time to savor the moment, reflect on how the world might change, and relax.

But history, it seems, had other plans.

A few minutes into our conversation we were interrupted by two Secret Service agents. The men said that the president-elect must be briefed at once on an issue of national security.

"We have a secure phone waiting for you, Mr. President."

There, behind the curtain, CIA officials informed President-elect Reagan via phone that the Soviets were believed to be in the process of shipping boxed fighter plane parts to Central America. Immediately, Reagan's jovial demeanor morphed into one of concern. In that moment the realities of the cold war and the threat of Communist expansion were no longer relegated to campaign rhetoric. They had become Ronald Reagan's responsibilities, and it had happened overnight.

It would be inaccurate to suggest that Reagan's commitment to facing down the former Soviet Union was the result of his backstage briefing. After all, he had been fighting communism going back to his days in Hollywood. But I have often felt that this episode was history's way of previewing future events. Reagan hadn't even been sworn in as president and already he was confronted with the work—indeed, threats—that lay ahead.

In the weeks preceding Reagan's inauguration, the majesty that is the formal transfer of power had already begun. Unlike other nations where changes in leadership are met with blood-shed and strife, for the most part, outgoing American presidents try to help, not hurt, their successors. This was true of President Carter and his staff. While they were understandably saddened about relinquishing the reins of power, they were committed to helping us get off to a solid beginning. And starting strong is important. Ever since President Franklin Delano Roosevelt invited observers to monitor his first one hundred days in office, presidential transitions have taken on great importance.

So before Reagan's inauguration, a group of us had been scheduled to meet with members of President Carter's staff. They would show us the White House and allow us to shadow them for the day while examining the facilities that would soon be under our care. At one point along the tour, we stopped on the South Lawn to take in the surroundings. I distinctly remember the way the sky looked that day. It was a clear ocean blue, and the sound of birds chirping could be heard in the distance—idyllic, to say the least. I turned to my friend Lyn Nofziger and said, "This has got to be one of most serene places on all the earth."

A battle-tested Washington veteran, Lyn had thought I was referring to Washington, D.C., and not the majestic setting that immediately surrounded us. "Dick, don't kid yourself," he warned. "This is one of the most vicious, cutthroat places on the planet. If you're smart, you will remind yourself of that every day you're here."

Lyn's words struck at the core of a debate that had been going on between my heart and my head over whether to accept Reagan's offer to join the White House as part of the president's inner circle.

On the one hand, I was deeply honored by the offer and my heart was saying yes. However, after analyzing the issue more closely, I wasn't so sure that was the best way to serve the president. For one thing, presidential pollsters have not historically been on the federal payroll. Instead, their services are usually routed through their respective political party machinery. But there was another, more strategic reason why I decided to turn down the president's request: I wanted Reagan to know that my counsel was independent of any ongoing turf battles that might arise within the White House.

So I suggested to the president-elect as well as the transition team that we set up a newly created White House Office of Planning and Strategy. I would arrange to be technically outside the White House structure, but installed someone from my group, Richard Beal, to head the office. This gave me the best of both worlds. I would have White House information resources at my disposal and the ability to keep an ear to the ground, while at the same time I could avoid getting caught in any circular firing squads.

And yet, one thing I learned long ago is that proximity is power. For my arrangement to serve Reagan well I needed assurance that my access to the president would remain unfettered. Graciously, Reagan ensured that it would. In fact, the reason he and I met "hundreds of times," as he once told an audience, was that he always kept both his door and his ear open to me.

When Reagan announced his staff selections, I felt even more confident about the decision I had made. Jim Baker was tapped to serve as chief of staff. Although Baker had cut his political teeth as a Bush man, and belonged to the "pragmatist" wing of the Republican establishment, he was and is one of the most experienced men in presidential politics. Ed Meese, a member of the so-called ideologue faction, was wisely selected to fashion policy and its implementation. Rounding out the troika was Mike Deaver, a man who understood Reagan's personal needs and impulses as well as anyone. Marty Anderson, Ed Rollins, Bill Clark, Dick Darman, David Gergen, and Lyn Nofziger completed the rest of the inner circle.

Someone recently asked me whether I ever regretted not joining the president's official staff. Honestly, it was one of the best decisions I've ever made, because Reagan told me that given my position he felt a level of comfort and ease sharing some of his private thoughts and concerns with me. He could tell me things without fear that our discussions would be used for personal leverage or position. When we sat alone in the Oval Office, he knew our conversations were confidential.

Now, that's not to say he was particularly wild about my decision not to formally join the executive staff. But I think he came to appreciate the flexibility it afforded him. He did, however, make one request. The president-elect asked me to serve as his director of Planning and Strategy for the Presidential Transition Committee, which was chaired by Ed Meese. As was his management style, Reagan set the objectives and left finding the most efficient way to achieve them up to us. My mandate was to map out the general political strategy and tactics of the first phase of President Reagan's 1981 administration in an "Initial Actions Report."

With the help of scores of committed staff members and Reagan's communicative hand steady on the wheel, the first two hundred days of the president's first term appeared to reach the primary objective articulated in the Initial Actions Report. That objective was, first and foremost, to take steps that would earn deeper respect and support from all Americans and to govern thereafter with the same goal. This would strengthen the Reagan White House and set into motion the long-term political changes that would keep the Reagan Revolution strong over the next two decades.

Getting off to a strong start also meant that Reagan would need to deliver an inaugural address that clearly and boldly communicated his vision of where he wanted to take America. And in this, he didn't disappoint. He spoke of freedom as a condition uniquely endowed by the hand of God, of curbing the size and scale of the federal government, and of how American heroes can often be found in the unlikeliest of places. As he said in his speech, "Those who say that we're in a time when there are no heroes, they just don't know where to look. You can see heroes every day going in and out of factory gates. . . . You meet heroes across a counter, and they're on both sides of that counter. . . . Their patriotism is quiet, but deep. Their values sustain our national life."

The 1981 inaugural address was also the first time an American president would deliver his speech on the West Front of the Capitol. Through the years, Reagan's chief visuals guru, Mike Deaver, had come up with some great ideas, but none better than his suggestion that the president speak while looking out over the Washington Mall. Not only was the scenery breathtaking, the speech was crafted in such a way that it read like stage directions for network television to follow. The net effect was a visual tour of Washington, D.C. From the Washington Monument, to the Jefferson Memorial, to the Lincoln Monument, the synergy between Reagan's words and the images of our nation's monumental treasures produced a visual grammar linking Ronald Reagan's ethos to that of the great presidents of America's past. Mike really outdid himself, but even he agrees it was Ronald Reagan's delivery that breathed life into the speech.

If you ever come across someone who questions Reagan's status as the Greatest Communicator, try this little experiment. Print them out a copy of Reagan's first inaugural address. Videotape the individual delivering Reagan's inaugural. Then play that tape side by side with Reagan's actual delivery. I guarantee the contrast will be stark.

The reason: a great speech in the hands of a novice is not a great speech. The confluence of two forces, content and delivery, is what creates powerful oratory. Reagan could deliver speeches that would have tied most speakers in knots. He knew how to make rhetoric come alive. He knew how to work the rhythms of a speech. The cadence, the rate, the dramatic pause—he owned them all. Sometimes while reading a line in an early speech draft I would say to myself, "Oh boy, that's going to fall flat." Then Reagan would stand up and deliver the line with a different point of emphasis, or a facial expression that brought new meaning to what he had said. Watching Ronald Reagan practice a speech was like watching Babe Ruth take batting practice. It was truly something to behold.

He also had a keen understanding of how a message or event would play in the public. One time, Meese, Deaver, Rollins, the president, and I were having lunch in the Oval Office. The White House dining staff, some of the best in the world, had set up a lovely round table complete with white linens and a floral arrangement made of fresh salmon-colored roses and light blue baby's breath. The menu that day included shrimp and clam chowder, salad, egg foo yong with crab legs, rice, and a strawberry sundae for dessert. About halfway through the meal, I started outlining some of the pitfalls I saw on the horizon. One of them involved unformed perceptions about Nancy. I said that symbols were important, and that the American people seemed to be indicating that they wanted to see more of her.

That's when someone pointed out that Nancy received little to no press coverage when she appeared in public without the president. Mike then said that what we needed were photo opportunities where the two of them could be seen together. He said someone had suggested that we have the president and first lady try a bicycle built for two. At that, the president laughed heartily. "That's pushing things too far," Reagan said. "She doesn't ride a bike and I'm not sure I could either."

As for the content of his speeches, Reagan was *always* involved in the drafting process. He was his own best speechwriter. And he was prolific. As Reagan archivists Kiron K. Skinner, Annelise Anderson, and Martin Anderson note in their collection of Reagan's letters, *Reagan: A Life in Letters*, throughout his career, Reagan may have penned upwards of ten thousand letters. Tony Dolan, one of the president's top wordsmiths and the author of the "Evil Empire" address, once said that the job of a Reagan speechwriter was to plagiarize the president's old speeches and give them back to him to deliver. Tony had it right. Reagan's communicative instincts were virtually always dead on. It made all our jobs that much easier.

But Reagan's ability to perform under the pressure of being at the podium was just part of what made him one of the greatest communicators. Indeed, it would be the president's ability to exhibit grace under fire on March 30, 1981, and the days that followed that would show the world the content of Ronald Reagan's character.

It had begun like any other day, except that it wasn't.

President Reagan had been scheduled to deliver a short speech at 2 p.m. to the National Conference of the Building and Construction Trades Department of the AFL-CIO, which was meeting just a little over a mile away from the White House at the Washington Hilton. The speech was to be short, no more than a half hour at most. Reagan's press secretary, Jim Brady, had made the fateful decision to join the president that day in place of his assistant, Larry Speakes.

After concluding his remarks, Reagan exited the hotel through a side door. He was joined by his personal aide Dave Fischer, Secret Service agent Jerry Parr, Mike Deaver, Jim Brady, press office aide David Prosperi, and Secret Service agent Tim McCarthy.

As a light drizzle descended from a darkened Washington sky, reporters and bystanders looked on as the seventy-year-old president—now on the job just seventy days—began walking toward the open door of his limousine. As he did, a reporter shouted in an effort to get the president's attention. Noticing Sam Donaldson in the distance, Reagan smiled and raised his left arm to wave. Deaver was on the president's left, Brady just a pace behind.

Ten feet away, a man Reagan had never seen before crouched into a shooter's position with his hands wrapped around a .22-caliber pistol.

The staccato sound of six Devastator bullets taking flight startled the president. Initially he thought they were firecrackers. But the acrid smell of gunpowder in the air told him otherwise.

Immediately, Jerry Parr's body did what it had been trained to do. While bending Reagan at the waist, Parr used his torso to shield the president before shoving him into the waiting limousine. When Parr's body landed on top of Reagan inside the car, the president, not realizing he had been hit, yelled at Parr. He thought the sheer weight of the Secret Service agent falling on him had broken one of his ribs. But the pain undulating through his body had been caused by a bullet, not Parr.

As the president's driver sped away from the scene, it appeared that the gunman had missed his target, or so Reagan and Parr thought. But Parr, fifty, a veteran of the Secret Service, continued to keep a watchful eye on his president. When Reagan started to cough, Parr gave him a handkerchief. As the president held it up to his lips, a crimson stain began spreading across the pocket square. Parr's eyes immediately darted to Reagan's mouth. A blood-filled froth was forming at the president's lips—a sure sign of a punctured lung.

Reagan had been hit.

The Secret Service agent immediately ordered the driver to go to George Washington University Hospital.

Meanwhile, back at the scene of the shooting, Jim Brady was battling for his life. A Devastator bullet had shattered a portion of his head. Doctors later thought he wouldn't make it. In addition, Agent Tim McCarthy had taken a bullet in the chest. As soon as he had heard the pops from the assailant's gun, McCarthy had leapt into the air, spreading his arms as wide as he could and blocking one of the shooter's six bullets. A policeman on the scene, Tom Delehanty, had also been shot in the neck.

As for the would-be assassin, he was now covered by the mass of men who had tackled him. The young man lying at the bottom of the pile had become obsessed with Jodie Foster's character in Martin Scorcese's film *Taxi Driver*, which told the story of a troubled taxi driver who decided to assassinate a political figure in an effort to win the affections of a woman on whom he had become fixated. By assassinating Ronald Reagan, the shooter thought he could win Jodie Foster's love. The shooter's name was John Hinckley.

As the president's limo screeched up to the hospital, Reagan wanted to project an air of decorum. He didn't want to alarm the country or, worse, Nancy. It still amazes me to this day, but, incredibly, Reagan gathered himself inside the limo, buttoned his jacket, and stepped out of the car. Unaided, he walked to the emergency room doors. As he passed out of the sight of television cameras, his knees buckled. The next thing he knew he was on a gurney being wheeled through the hospital. His breathing now shallow, the president began fading in and out of consciousness. The next face he saw belonged to Nancy.

He looked at her and said, "Honey, I forgot to duck." It was an old line used by boxer Jack Dempsey following his loss to Gene Tunney in a heavyweight bout. It was also the first of many examples of Reagan's use of humor to comfort those around him. He was battling for his life, and all he could think about was offering solace to others.

When one of his doctors told him they would have to operate, Reagan looked up at him and said, "I hope you're a Republican." The surgeon chuckled and said, "Today, Mr. President, we're all Republicans."

It was later determined that one of Hinckley's Devastator bullets had ricocheted off the president's limo, flattened into a shape like a miniature buzz-saw blade, and entered Reagan's body just under his left armpit. For a time, doctors couldn't find the entry wound. They would soon make a shocking discovery.

Hinckley's bullet was lodged one inch from the president's heart.

One inch—the equivalent of six lines of type on this page. That's all that separated the fortieth president from death.

What if he had shaken one more hand? What if he had leaned forward another inch? What if Hinckley had aimed an inch to either side? What if Parr had reacted a split second slower?

What if?

As Reagan learned the condition of the other men, he closed his eyes and prayed. In his conversation with God, he included what some might consider an unlikely individual—his would-be assassin. As Reagan would later write in his autobiography, *An American Life*, "I didn't feel I could ask God's help to heal Jim, the others, and myself, and at the same time feel hatred for the man who had shot us, so I silently asked God to help him deal with whatever demons had led him to shoot us."

While Reagan was continuing his recovery, his nurse would periodically check on him. One particular day, she came in to find the president of the United States on the floor of his bathroom on his hands and knees. The leader of the free world had spilled some water and was mopping it up. It turns out that Reagan was worried his nurse would be blamed for the wet floor, and he didn't want her to get in trouble.

Miraculously, all four of the men hit by Hinckley's bullets would survive. Jim Brady, however, would suffer the most. Indeed, Jim will live out the rest of his life confined to a wheelchair. In an interview following Reagan's death, Brady said that he considers having served the president the highest honor and privilege of his life. Amazing words from a man who paid dearly for serving his country and his president.

Following the assassination attempt, none of us who worked alongside the president would ever look at his travel schedule or surroundings in the same way. Like Nancy, I found myself noticing dangers I hadn't before. For example, I recall the feeling that fell over me during a meeting in the Oval Office with Baker, Meese, Deaver, and the president when my eye picked up something I had never observed. Covering the windows surrounding the president's desk was a heavy dark green bulletproof glass shield designed to protect him in the event of a sniper attack. It cast a somber note and represented a jarring contrast with the comfortable decor of the rest of the room— a constant reminder of the high costs leadership sometimes exacts.

After he was released from the hospital, Reagan and I would have our first meeting in the Oval Office since the shooting. It was just the two of us, and I was eager to see him in familiar surroundings.

We sat beside the fireplace visiting with one another. Ever since 1968, we had felt comfortable discussing matters of family and faith. It was a unique dimension of our relationship, one he always let me know he appreciated. There was a spiritual symmetry there, and on this day I sensed Reagan had something he wanted to tell me.

"Dick, you know, I feel like the man upstairs was looking out for me. I think He spared me for a reason. I'm not sure why. But I've decided that whatever time I have left on this earth, I will try to serve Him any way I can."

As long as I live, I shall never forget those words.

Reagan's actions in the wake of the assassination attempt produced an outpouring of public support. The president had become a living embodiment of Ernest Hemingway's definition of courage as "grace under pressure." The American people had seen their newly elected president in the direst of circumstances, and they liked what they saw. Instead of melodrama, Reagan offered levity. Instead of focusing on himself, Reagan expressed concern for others.

But it remained to be seen whether this wellspring of

goodwill would last. The president needed to prove his ability to lead in the policy arena.

On July 29, 1981, Reagan took his first step in that direction when his 25 percent tax cut was approved by Congress. Later tax bills would provide even greater relief to American families, but to have won a major economic policy initiative in his first seven months in office was a solid achievement. It was also the beginning of a new approach to stimulating economic investment and growth.

When most politicians and economists sit around discussing tax policy, they lard their conversations with numbers, theories, and the kind of jargon most people find mind-numbingly boring. I have to plead guilty to this. My graduate school days in the economics department at Berkeley had infected me with this disease.

Reagan had studied economics too. But he had somehow avoided the plague that the rest of us suffered from. He knew how to talk about dollars and cents in a way that showed Americans he understood what they understood: money is meaningless. What money *represents* is priceless.

In the first days of 1981, Reagan sat down and wrote out an early draft of what would later become his February 5, 1981, address to the nation on economic policy. Pay close attention to the communicative brilliance rushing just beneath the surface of his statement about taxes and the economy.

> I'm not going to subject you to the jumble of charts and figures and economic jargon of that audit, but rather will try to explain where we are, how we got there, and how we can get back. . . .
>
> There are seven million Americans caught up in the personal indignity and human tragedy of unemployment. If they stood in a line, allowing three feet for each person, the line would reach from the coast of Maine to California.

Let me try to put this in personal terms. Here is a dollar such as you earned, spent, or saved in 1960. Here is quarter, a dime, and a penny—thirty-six cents. Thirty-six cents is what this 1960 dollar is worth today. And if the present inflation rate should continue a couple of more years that dollar of 1960 will be worth a dime.

Many Democrats think that all Republicans care about is money. They call the GOP the party of the rich—one big fat country club. Quite honestly, before Ronald Reagan came along it was easy to see why Democrats had gotten away with this silliness for as long as they had. Republicans spoke about money and taxes using the same cold, sterile language that fills textbooks.

It took the likes of Ronald Reagan to teach us how to discuss monetary matters in ways that were personally relevant. You see, the reason Reagan was so fixated on taxes, deregulation, and unleashing the power of the marketplace had absolutely nothing to do with greed. Quite the reverse! Reagan understood what keeping more of one's money represented. It meant more time with family, sending a child to college, taking a family vacation, owning a home, having a job that provided a sense of dignity and pride in oneself—the very things he wrote about in his speech. These were the reasons he fought so hard for tax relief. He wasn't concerned about millionaires. He was looking out for the little guy, and people sensed it when he spoke.

I remember one time I was in the Oval Office with the president and Don Regan, the former treasury secretary who would later become Reagan's chief of staff during the second term. Regan was a man of Wall Street and had run among the corporate crowd all his life. Somehow we got on the subject of the Philippine leader Ferdinand Marcos and his limitless wealth. Marcos's wife, Imelda, had gained international notoriety when it was revealed that she owned something in excess of three hundred pairs of shoes.

During the conversation the president posed a rhetorical question: "What can you possibly do more once you have four to five million dollars?" I glanced at Don Regan, who was now rolling his eyes slightly at the president's comment. But I didn't see it the way Don did. I thought this somewhat innocent suggestion reflected the president's strong view that holding political power—as well as economic power—is a stewardship. Reagan thought the least Marcos could do was apply some of his personal fortune to help his own country.

A couple days after the president's tax bill had passed, the president, Vice President Bush, Ed Rollins, Lyn Nofziger, Ed Meese, and I all met in the Oval Office. Reagan had on his light beige suit, the one he always seemed to prefer during the summer months. I made a point of sitting to his left. It's a little-known fact, but Reagan had lost virtually all ability to hear in his right ear during a shootout scene in the movie *Code of the Secret Service*. You could sometimes get a sense of how well a person knew Reagan by where he decided to sit if given his choice of chairs.

The president asked me to open the meeting. I did so by congratulating him on the passage of the tax bill. It had sent an important message to the American people: Reagan could enact his agenda. After years of gridlock and inaction, the tax bill was proof that the president was taking action to combat the recession.

Before we got down to business, Reagan passed the traditional jar of jelly beans. As we each took some, the president said he used to simply take a handful but that he had since become a picker and a chooser—banana and peanut butter being his favorite flavors. When the jar got around to Bush, the vice president rued the fact that there were no black jelly beans. Reagan explained that they were all "natural" flavors. Bush responded, "Well, I hope that won't appear to be discriminatory to anyone."

I told the president that the passage of the tax bill was historic because it made good on his mandate to lead while at the same time increasing positive perceptions of the Republican Party. I quoted Emerson to the effect that "all political systems, wherever they might be, can be divided into just two parties—the party of memory and the party of hope." Reagan responded that he surely felt that the Democrats had become the party of memory and that's all that they were offering—the memory of FDR and the social programs he initiated. I reminded him of my recent poll findings that while Americans were more hopeful, there remained pockets of the electorate—namely blacks—who didn't share that sense of optimism.

Reagan said he was eager to begin initiating the creation of Jack Kemp's "enterprise zones," a policy initiative designed to provide economic assistance to those businesses and individuals willing to invest in the inner cities. The president remarked that while he understood why many younger black Americans felt a sense of hopelessness, he was saddened that many were unaware of the amazing strides in civil rights that had occurred over his lifetime. He said that only two decades ago when he was in the movie industry, some of the highest-paid black entertainers—the very best in the business—were forced to stay in the shabbiest hotels. He said he could well remember being in the South when he represented General Electric and seeing the separate drinking, eating, and bathroom facilities. And yet, for those who had not lived through that period, Reagan said he could understand easily why younger blacks didn't share his hope for continued racial healing.

In the fall of 1981, I reviewed how the president's economic policy and the tax cuts had been perceived by the American people. Three out of every four Americans felt that at least half of the Reagan economic program had been implemented. Overall, his policies had been well received. Fifty-nine percent believed his economic plan would reduce inflation, 58 percent called the plan "fair," and 57 percent said it would increase productivity. A strong majority of Americans also felt

Reagan had "the strong leadership qualities this country needs," was "trustworthy," and would continue being "effective in getting things done."

But most importantly, Reagan's ability to communicate matters of dollars and cents had begun erasing the negative stereotypes Republicans had been battling for years. A large random sample of Americans were asked whether they thought the statements "shows too much business favoritism" and "does not care enough about the needs of the elderly and poor" applied to Ronald Reagan. Almost every category of voter rejected these two descriptions. The reason? Reagan spoke from the heart. He cared about the poor because he had grown up poor himself. Moreover, he understood that for most Americans economic policy isn't some abstract, academic exercise. It's personal. It's immediate. When he spoke about such things, he did so in ways that were intensely relevant—ways that showed he cared.

As caring and compassionate as Ronald Reagan was about the economic needs of individual Americans, nothing, and I mean *nothing*, would prevent him from doing what he believed was in the best interests of the country. Yes, you could say that he was as strong as he was sensitive.

That was certainly the case when 12,000 members of the Professional Air Traffic Controllers Organization (PATCO) union decided to strike in August 1981—an action that was prohibited by federal law. Many believed that public employees going on strike sacrificed the good of the whole for the benefit of the few, and Reagan wouldn't stand for it. So he gave the strikers forty-eight hours to return to work. When they defied his orders, despite the fact that PATCO had actually backed him during his 1980 presidential campaign, Reagan remorsefully, yet firmly, announced that these individuals were no longer public employees.

Reagan was decisive, and his willingness to back up his

words with action confirmed that he meant what he said. The standoff with PATCO was a test of the president's resolve, and he had passed with flying colors. Three weeks after his decision, I surveyed the American public to see whether they approved of Ronald Reagan's handling of the situation. By an overwhelming 71 percent, the American people agreed with the president's decision. What's more, the episode had dealt a body blow to the perceptions of unions. For example, in January of 1981, 53 percent of those asked said public employees should have the right to strike. By August, that number had plummeted to 35 percent.

The president took no joy in letting 12,000 workers go. As I mentioned earlier, Reagan hated to fire anyone. But this facet of the president's personality had made his decision that much more impressive. He would not allow a select few to thwart the good of the whole. Still young in his presidency, Ronald Reagan proved to all watching that his words were real. He didn't bluff. When he said something, he meant it.

And perhaps that is why Reagan's words delivered on March 8, 1983, created such a stir among his critics in America and in other countries as well. Reagan had done the unthinkable. He had called a spade a spade. He had told the truth. He had called the Soviet Union an "evil empire."

Reagan speechwriter Tony Dolan, a brilliant wordsmith, deep thinker, and Pulitzer Prize–winning author, had been assigned to write the president's remarks for his appearance at the National Association of Evangelicals in Orlando, Florida. Dolan and the president worked together closely on the speech, encountering opposition from some in the administration. Still, Reagan pressed on.

When Reagan was finished delivering the address, two things became immediately clear. First, the force and depth of his words had connected with the Christian community in a way unmatched by any other American president in recent memory. And second, Reagan's brand of moral absolutism had infuriated both the European elite as well as many American liberals.

Reagan had struck his rhetorical staff against the political earth and ripped open a fissure separating liberals from conservatives. The president's words were a perfect example of the bifurcation between conservative and liberal oratory, which is best summarized as the difference between moral clarity and something liberals like to call "nuance." Reagan spoke the language of the "black hat" versus the "white hat," good versus evil—offenses of the worst kind in the eyes of liberals. He did so not in a spirit of haughty arrogance or self-righteousness, but rather in a humble spirit of moral certainty and forthrightness of spirit. Most egregious of all, he had dared to infuse his faith in God into the text of his speech.

Gray—not black and white—is the rhetorical hue of choice for the liberal. According to this way of seeing the world, no personal choice is necessarily more or less virtuous. Instead, choices in personal behavior are just that, choices—options among a host of many. For the liberal, to state otherwise is to be uncouth and uncivilized.

Never mind that what Reagan was saying about the brutality of the Soviet regime was in fact true. Never mind that literally millions of citizens had been slaughtered at the hands of totalitarian aggression. Never mind that many former political prisoners—lovers of freedom—such as Aleksandr Solzhenitsyn, who had endured life in the gulags, were nodding in agreement as Reagan spoke his words of truth. These minor details mattered little.

The *real* offense, according to Reagan's detractors, was that an American president would have the audacity to hold aloft his religious faith in the context of a speech that had serious policy implications. And he had done so without apology or equivocation. This, in the mind of many liberals, was unthinkable, brutish behavior.

If you want to understand how Ronald Reagan's faith and

political philosophy drove the words he spoke, you need to read the following excerpt from "Evil Empire." I realize that when reading a book it is sometimes tempting to skip over block quotes. But don't—at least not the extract below.

There is sin and evil in the world, and we're enjoined by Scripture and the Lord Jesus to oppose it with all our might. Our nation, too, has a legacy of evil with which it must deal. The glory of this land has been its capacity for transcending the moral evils of our past. For example, the long struggle of minority citizens for equal rights, once a source of disunity and civil war, is now a point of pride for all Americans. We must never go back. There is no room for racism, anti-Semitism, or other forms of ethnic and racial hatred in this country. . . .

Especially in this century, America has kept alight the torch of freedom, but not just for ourselves but for millions of others around the world. . . .

And this brings me to my final point today. During my first press conference as president, in answer to a direct question, I point out that, as good Marxist-Leninists, the Soviet leaders have openly and publicly declared that the only morality they recognize is that which will further their cause, which is world revolution. . . .

We will never give away our freedom. We will never abandon our belief in God. And we will never stop searching for a genuine peace. . . . The reality is that we must find peace through strength. . . .

Yes, let us pray for the salvation of all of those who live in that totalitarian darkness—pray they will discover the joy of knowing God. But until they do, let us be aware that while they preach the supremacy of the state, declare its omnipotence over individual man, and predict its eventual domination of all peoples on the earth, they are the focus of evil in the modern world. . . .

So, in your discussions of the nuclear freeze proposals, I urge you to beware the temptation of pride—the temptation of blithely declaring yourselves above it all and label both sides equally at fault, to ignore the facts of history and the aggressive impulses of an evil empire, to simply call the arms race a giant misunderstanding and thereby remove yourself from the struggle between right and wrong and good and evil. . . .

The real crisis we face today is a spiritual one; at root, it is a test of moral will and faith. . . .

I believe that communism is another sad, bizarre chapter in human history whose last pages even now are being written. . . .

One of our Founding Fathers, Thomas Paine, said, "We have it within our power to begin the world over again." We can do it, doing together what no one church could do by itself.

God bless you, and thank you very much.

Fortunately for the world, Ronald Reagan was uniquely suited to confront communism. The reason? Well, there were several. But chief among them was Reagan's belief that communism was a form of modern-day slavery. This conviction was at the core of the Reagan vision.

The word "vision" has become the cultural equivalent of elevator music—its ubiquity has rendered it meaningless. Quite literally, vision means "the ability to see." But *what* a person sees and how he or she talks about it are what differentiates those who lead from those who are led. Compelling visions are like masterpieces of art: although they depict scenes and objects of varied kinds, they are created using similar tools—canvas, paint, brush.

Ronald Reagan's vision came as the result of answering a simple question: How will my leadership positively change others' reality, and what will that new reality look like? Notice the importance of the phrase "look like." Because vision involves sight, Reagan understood that an audience must be able to see in their mind's eye just what a leader's vision would look like if carried to completion. Many would-be leaders think this means their vision should involve some long, complex tangle of intricately layered ideas expressed in florid language. Not so. What Ronald Reagan taught me is that the best vision statements are simple and easy to understand. Reagan's vision was threefold: restore America's confidence in itself, encourage economic growth without inflation, and lift the draconian sword of Mutually Assured Destruction (MAD) through arms reduction and the normalization of relations with the Soviet Union. To animate his dream, and thereby boost the visual nature of his vision, Reagan employed a metaphor—an exemplifying image—that crystallized his bold dream for his audience: the city on a hill.

The impressive thing about Ronald Reagan's vision, the thing that gave it muscle, was that it went unchanged throughout his political career. Through the years he never vacillated. He remained steady in an unstable world, consistent through times of change. In our age of waffling politicians, doublespeak, and endless equivocation, Ronald Reagan's steadfast spirit was a refreshing departure from the norm.

The other great thing about Ronald Reagan's unwavering spirit was . . . it drove his political opponents nuts! They tried everything to get him to cave in. But he never did. One of their favorite tactics was to credit my data and me with having told the president what to say. But the fact is, Ronald Reagan was talking about his vision *long* before I became his chief strategist and pollster. Consider the following speech excerpt:

Standing on the tiny deck of the *Arabella* in 1630 off the Massachusetts coast, John Winthrop said, "We will be as a city upon a hill. The eyes of all people are upon us, so that if we deal falsely with our God in this work we have undertaken and so cause Him to withdraw His present help from us, we shall be made a story and a byword throughout the world.". . . We cannot escape our destiny, nor should we try to do so. The leadership of the free world was thrust upon us two centuries ago in that little hall of Philadelphia.

We are indeed, and we are today, the last best hope of man on earth.

That speech was delivered January 25, 1974.

Even when his time in the White House was up, the president was *still* communicating his vision. Here is how Reagan described the vision he had spoken about throughout his political life while delivering his 1989 farewell address.

The past few days when I've been at that window upstairs, I've thought a bit of the "shining city upon a hill." The phrase comes from John Winthrop, who wrote it to describe the America he imagined. What he imagined was important because he was an early Pilgrim, an early freedom man. . . . In my mind [America] was a tall, proud city built on rocks stronger than oceans, windswept, God-blessed, and teeming with people of all kinds living in harmony and peace; a city with free ports that hummed with commerce and creativity. And if there had to be city walls, the walls had doors and the doors were open to anyone with the will and the heart to get here. That's how I saw it, and see it still.

And how stands the city on this winter night? More prosperous, more secure, and happier than it was eight years ago. But more than that: After two hundred years, two centuries, she still stands strong and true on the granite ridge, and her glow has held steady no matter what storm. And she's still a beacon, still a magnet for all who must have freedom, for all the pilgrims from all the lost places who are hurtling through the darkness, toward home.

Almost fifteen years later to the day, Reagan's vision had remained unchanged—same city, same hill. It was John Winthrop, not Ronald Reagan, who had originally conceived of "a city on a hill." And let's face it, the phrase wasn't exactly bursting with immediacy—it was conceived in 1630! But it was Ronald Reagan who dusted off that oratorical gem, held it up to the light of his values, and cast a sparkling vision for Americans to follow. He didn't just repeat ragged mantras like so many politicians do. He took something old and made it new.

It's also important to notice that Reagan's statement about the shining city on a hill represents much more than mere eloquence. The metaphor served a strategic purpose. It drove home the three elements of Reagan's broader vision I mentioned earlier.

For example, "A tall proud city" echoed Reagan's vision to "restore America's confidence in itself." "A city with free ports that hummed with commerce and creativity" reinforced his desire to "encourage economic growth without inflation." "Built on rocks stronger than oceans, wind-swept, God-blessed, and teeming with people of all kinds living in harmony and peace . . . and if there had to be city walls, the walls had doors and the doors were open" reflected Reagan's desire to "Lift the draconian nuclear sword of MAD through arms reduction and the normalization of relations with the former Soviet Union."

And so Reagan's vision was as cogent as it was clear. Because he held fast to his principles, his rhetoric projected an air of confidence and consistency at a time of American self-doubt, a time when "malaise" had gripped the nation. His laser-like focus on achieving his tripartite vision was impressive, and he possessed a unique understanding that these three goals were, in many ways, inextricably linked. Yet while Reagan considered all three components important, one of these meant the most to him personally.

Presidential historians grapple constantly with the question of presidential legacy. It is one of those things that everyone who works in a White House thinks about but seldom discusses. Presidents play this game too. Most refrain from mentioning the L word until their final days in office or until their post-presidency. And even then, they do so reluctantly.

Reagan was similar in this respect. Nothing made him more uncomfortable than talking about himself. He had entered office with a mission, a vision of what he hoped to accomplish. He hadn't sought the presidency for fame or fortune. Hollywood had already given him both. No, Reagan wanted to be president for a simple reason: he wanted to transform the world. He wanted to reshape the way future Americans would live. And he knew exactly what he wanted to be remembered for.

I know because he told me so.

A defining moment that showed me how Ronald Reagan viewed his role as commander in chief came just as his economic policies were beginning to kick in and produce what would later become unprecedented economic growth. One evening, Nancy, the president, and I were meeting in the first family's private residence in the White House. In the midst of our discussion about the encouraging economic successes of the day, out of nowhere, Reagan interrupted me in midsentence.

"Dick, you know what I *really* want to be remembered for?" he asked.

The nostalgic lilt in his voice let me know that there wasn't a punch line waiting on the other end. He was being serious, his tone contemplative.

"No, Mr. President, what is it that you want to be remembered for?" I asked.

"I want to be remembered as the president of the United

States who brought a sense and reality of peace and security. I want to eliminate that awful fear that each of us feels sometimes when we get up in the morning knowing that the world could be destroyed through a nuclear holocaust."

In all our years together, I had never heard him speak of his own legacy this way. It was almost as if he just needed to hear himself say it out loud. That he would open himself up this way and share his heart in such striking language touched me deeply.

I've since reflected on that moment up in the private residence and why Reagan felt the need to verbalize his deepest desires. I have concluded that, at the time of this writing, there are only five men alive today who understand what it's like to carry a credit card in your pocket with codes that have the power to end human civilization. None of us can fully appreciate the weight that rests on a president's shoulders.

Also, I think it's hard for young people to fully appreciate the degree to which the cold war and, specifically, the Soviet military threat affected those of us who grew up during that period. For example, in the fall of 1983 I asked Americans the following question: "Do you believe that the military threat from the Soviet Union is constantly growing and presents a real immediate danger to the United States, or not?" A jaw-dropping 77 percent of those polled said the Soviets represented an immediate danger. After having grown up crawling under school desks during bomb drills, Americans had come to see the threat posed by the Soviet Union as both pervasive and proximate.

But even before becoming president, Reagan had been haunted by the prospects of nuclear annihilation. In his 1964 speech for Barry Goldwater, he told America that we faced "a time for choosing." The choice was clear, said Reagan. "We will preserve for our children this, the last best hope for man on earth, or we will sentence them to take the last step into a thousand years of darkness."

So, hearing him verbalize his desired legacy was telling not because I was unaware of the president's passion for peace, but because it revealed just how completely he had internalized his vision. In his own mind, he had defined his legacy in terms of leaving the world safer than he found it. Reagan's early days as a lifeguard had become a prescient symbol. More than saving seventy-seven lives in Rock River, the president longed to provide security for all the inhabitants of the world.

It was a lofty vision, to be sure. But that night in the private residence convinced me that this was a man who was *obsessed* with peace. It remains one of the great ironies of the Reagan legacy. Here was a president who yearned for a more peaceful world. And yet his political opponents tried to make him out to be a warmongering cowboy. Even following his death, many of those same voices of dissent were left scratching their heads in disbelief. This, you may recall, was the crowd that used to call Reagan the "Teflon president." To this day they can't understand why their charges never stuck.

Well, I'll tell you why they didn't stick. They weren't true! Reagan's optimism for the future and passion for peace belied his detractors' arguments. Their confusion stemmed from their inability—unwillingness, perhaps—to understand that peace is best achieved through strength. And it was this element of Reagan's peace equation—strength—that caused consternation and hand-wringing among those who fought against the president's bold vision for America.

You may recall that during Reagan's presidency the so-called nuclear freeze movement had built up a good head of steam. This was the group who favored halting American production of nuclear weapons regardless of whether the Soviets did the same. In other words, they wanted the United States to disarm unilaterally.

Mention the phrase "nuclear freeze" today around the liberals and media who supported it at the time and you are likely to hear dismissive chuckles, the kind that say, "Well, we were all once naïve and silly." Yet back then, these same individuals demanded that the "movement" be treated with solemnity and respect.

I kept a careful eye on the nuclear freeze issue. On November 20, 1983, ABC decided to air a television movie called *The Day After* about the ravages of fallout in the wake of a nuclear incident. The movie provided a gripping and emotional look at the issue, and I was sensitive to the impact images and popular culture could have on the formation of public opinion. So following the publicity and airing of the film I polled Americans about their views on a unilateral nuclear freeze. Initially, the movie seemed to have made some impact on American attitudes, particularly among women who had watched it.

Still, on the big question of whether Americans favored or opposed unilaterally freezing the production of nuclear weapons, 60 percent agreed with the president's position that this would be ill-advised. Consistent with their opposition to a unilateral destruction of our nuclear arsenal, 63 percent of respondents also agreed with the statement "The best way to guarantee peace is for the U.S. to be so strong that no one will dare attack us," a position Ronald Reagan had been espousing for years.

However, despite all the hype, the president wasted little time worrying about the voices of dissent. At some level, I suppose he believed them well-intentioned souls who, just like him, merely longed for peace, even if they did so in a way that was illogical and dangerous. No, the thing that really offended Ronald Reagan wasn't protestors, it was a national security strategy premised on a set of cynical, antiquated, theoretical assumptions. The name of that construct was Mutually Assured Destruction (MAD).

In Reagan's view, the United States' policy of nuclear deterrence—MAD—dangled from a dangerous expectation: if two countries possess nuclear arsenals capable of annihilating each other, neither will. For Reagan, that wasn't good enough. On numerous occasions the president let me know how mad MAD made him. He believed that relying on the good graces of potentially hostile nations was a fool's wager. Placing the sovereignty and security of America in the hands of those who had proven themselves untrustworthy was unacceptable. He dreamed of something greater. President Reagan desired *sustainable* world peace.

Enter the Strategic Defense Initiative (SDI). The concept behind SDI was simple: create a defense system capable of knocking nuclear missiles out of the sky before they could reach their intended targets. Once it was built, share the technology with all nations so as to achieve global security.

The sheer grandeur of Reagan's vision drew cackles from some quarters. The very notion of a "space shield" seemed like the stuff of Hollywood, not 1600 Pennsylvania Avenue. It wasn't long before Democrats and the media branded SDI with what they hoped would be a derisive label. Instead of SDI, they called it "Star Wars."

Oddly enough, I welcomed the phrase. Calling the proposal Star Wars helped Americans visualize the concept in a way that SDI just couldn't. In fact, when polling on the issue, I would often replace "SDI" with "Star Wars" when devising questions because the overwhelming majority of Americans (81 percent) said they had heard the program referred to in this way. The joke ended up being on the president's opponents, not Reagan.

But regardless of what one called it, one group that wasn't laughing was the Soviets. Despite the president's offer to share any emerging technology, the former Soviet Union feared that were the United States able to develop a system capable of protecting itself from nuclear attack, America would catapult itself into a position of global dominance, thereby rendering the former Soviet Union's massive nuclear arsenal irrelevant. Whether the technology was operable was irrelevant. The

Russians had determined that it was, and that was all that mattered.

Yet domination was the last thing Reagan was interested in. The president believed that America's story was one of liberty and freedom, not oppression. SDI was about defense, not offense. Still, adversaries doubted his intentions. So, on March 23, 1983, President Reagan laid out his bold vision for a more peaceful world in a nationally televised speech. As he announced his decision to begin conducting research on SDI, he communicated a "can-do" message rooted in hope.

> Let me share with you a vision of the future which offers hope. It is that we embark on a program to counter the awesome Soviet missile threat with measures that are defensive. . . .
>
> What if free people could live secure in the knowledge that their security did not rest upon the threat of instant U.S. retaliation to deter a Soviet attack, that we could intercept and destroy strategic ballistic missiles before they reached our own soil or that of our allies?
>
> I know this is a formidable, technical task, one that may not be accomplished before the end of this century. Yet, current technology has attained a level of sophistication where it's reasonable for us to begin this effort. It will take years, probably decades of effort on many fronts. There will be failures and setbacks, just as there will be successes and breakthroughs. But isn't it worth every investment necessary to free the world from the threat of nuclear war? We know it is. . . .
>
> Proceeding boldly with these new technologies, we can significantly reduce any incentive that the Soviet Union may have to threaten attack against the United States or its allies. . . .
>
> I call upon the scientific community in our country, those who gave us nuclear weapons, to turn their great

talents now to the cause of mankind and world peace, to give us the means of rendering these nuclear weapons impotent and obsolete. . . .

My fellow Americans, tonight we're launching an effort which holds the promise of changing the course of human history. There will be risks, and results take time. But I believe we can do it. As we cross this threshold, I ask for your prayers and your support.

Thank you, good night, and God bless you.

By proposing a new approach for achieving peace, Reagan's vision sparked the American imagination. Moreover, the very notion that the United States would devise such technology and then share it with the world conveyed a level of self-confidence that shook Soviet leaders to their core and ultimately hastened the end of the cold war. But what about Americans? Had Reagan's revolutionary proposal nudged voters toward his vision?

Yes.

After three years of listening to Ronald Reagan explain his bold vision of a defense system capable of preventing an intercontinental ballistic missile attack, 63 percent of Americans approved of the president's proposed SDI. As it turned out, "Star Wars" wasn't only the name of a popular motion picture, it also became the phrase that a majority of Americans associated with Reagan's plan to help keep the peace and end the cold war—the very thing Ronald Reagan told me he wanted to be remembered for.

Reagan accomplished so much good during that first term in office. From the beauty of his inaugural address, surviving the assassination attempt, passing his first tax bill, handling the PATCO strike, and remaining steadfast in the face of communism in an effort to foster his dream of peace, Reagan had modeled effective leadership. And yet for all his accomplishments, in the early part of 1983, I sensed potential trouble rumbling in the distance—the kind of trouble that, if gone uncorrected, could potentially derail his chances at reelection.

Sound strategy always involves keeping focused on the future while remaining aware of the past. A lover of presidential history, I was well aware of the historical precedent for presidents entering their third year in office. And it wasn't a pretty picture.

The reasons for this are myriad. First, midterm congressional elections almost always benefit the party out of presidential power. Voters of the opposition party tend to be more energized because of their outsider status. So, with the congressional balance of power tipping in the direction of the political party opposite the president's, enacting one's agenda is made that much more difficult.

Also, the third year of a president's term is when other potential candidates begin sizing up the electoral landscape to see whether they will throw their hat in the ring. Wanting to stake out their positions and draw contrast between themselves and the incumbent president, these individuals often become much more vocal in their opposition.

But these were "fixed" obstacles, things we could expect. The thing that concerned me most was the erosion of President Reagan's perceptual strengths. Qualities like "trustworthiness" and "strong leadership qualities," elements that had long been some of his strongest assets, were beginning to show signs of slippage. So on December 8, 1982, I drafted a twelve-page memorandum for the president titled "Political Challenges We Face in 1983 and Beyond."

At that time, Reagan was suffering politically because of a sluggish economic recovery. Understandably, people were anxious to see concrete signs of economic improvement. The Democrats had hammered at this theme to great effect during the 1982 midterm congressional races. With twenty-six fewer Republicans in the House of Representatives, as well as the loss of eleven state legislatures, the political-legislative environment had become much tougher.

Another winning theme for the Democrats had been the charge that the Reagan administration's policies were "unfair." I was especially sensitive to this accusation because fairness remains a core American value.

Given all this, I drafted my memo to the president in candid, stark language. Although Reagan hadn't yet formally decided to run for reelection, the memo was written with an eye toward the future. It began, "The next six months promise to be the most critical period of your presidency. Regardless of whether or not you decide to run for reelection in 1984, what is done now will determine whether your policies will remain in force over the next two decades and open a new era of freedom and opportunity for Americans, or whether your policies will give way to the old agendas of the past."

I then cataloged the myriad steps I believed the president needed to take to position himself for success. The memo concluded with a warning. While we were successful in 1981 at pushing through Congress many of his legislative programs, we had seemed to lose our touch entering 1983. I proposed that we refocus and begin strategizing for success. "Only by doing these things in 1983," the last line read, "can we keep the Reagan Revolution alive for another two decades."

In addition to the expected challenges all presidents face in their third year in office, Reagan would be forced to confront a series of unexpected crises in foreign policy. As a result, our usual Oval Office sessions during this period took on even greater importance.

The first of these sessions took place on January 12, 1983. I arrived at the Oval Office about ten minutes early and spoke with Ed Meese in the outer office. Then I dialed up Nancy and chatted with her on the phone a few minutes while we waited for Baker to arrive. Jim joined us and we all went in to meet with the president. A fire crackled in the fireplace. I sat at the left side of the president's desk.

I began by telling Ronald Reagan that, as always, I had good news and bad news to report. I started with the latter. I reported that 64 percent of Americans thought the country was on the wrong track. That number was largely a reflection of negative perceptions about the economy. For the first time since I had began measuring his job approval rating, more people disapproved of the job he was doing than approved. When I said that, Reagan looked up with a rather stern look on his face and simply said, "Hmmm." I think it shocked him and probably hurt a little bit. He was always sensitive to the way others felt about him, and he knew that his leadership hinged on his ability to marshal positive perceptions toward his goals.

At the end of our meeting I handed the president the results of my most recent survey. He stood, shook my hand, looked at me a little warily, and said, "Dick, when I get through reading all that, am I going to be happy or sad?"

"Mr. President," I replied, "we're going to have a rough time over the next sixty or ninety days. But given a little break with Congress and the economy, I think we're going to see things improving."

I wished the president a happy new year. Deaver chuckled and said, "I hope it is!"

At the end of March, I analyzed the specific forces of erosion working against the president. The usual gang—Baker, Meese, Deaver, the president, and myself—met in the Oval Office to discuss my findings. National Security Adviser Bill Clark sat in on that meeting as well. The most animated discussion came in response to one of my tables discussing the president's various image characteristics and the fact that we were experiencing strong erosion on what were typically three of Reagan's strongest perceptual assets: "effective in getting things done," "has strong leadership this country needs," and "trustworthy." Reagan said he knew the source of the deterioration.

"The problem is this whole thing about who makes decisions in the White House," the president said.

He had it exactly right.

Fifty-six percent of those asked said they believed that senior White House aides, not the president himself, were responsible for making major decisions. When I relayed this statistic, Reagan simply shook his head in disbelief. He then paraphrased a quote from Abraham Lincoln about how even if a thousand angels believe you were right, ultimately you are still the only one to know.

The notion that Reagan was somehow uninvolved or, worse, unaware of the events happening in the White House is both true *and* false. Let me explain. Reagan wasn't a micromanager. He wasn't terribly interested in what color the stationery was, or about organizational charts, or about the minutiae involved in a decision. That wasn't what excited him. He was a visionary, and visionaries are seldom drawn to detail. Reagan would tell us what his goals were, what he wanted us to do, and then he would expect us to go out and find the best way to achieve his objectives. Those closest to him often knew his impulses well enough to anticipate what he wanted. But assuming too much could be dangerous, and there were some instances when Reagan's managerial style of delegation produced unintended consequences. Still, overall, it was an effective way for him to run the White House.

My statistic about a majority of Americans thinking he was not the key decision maker had irked him, but there was also good news to report. Voters had started to see the economy in a much more favorable light. I felt strongly that the issue of fairness and the economy improving were directly linked to one another. Once we felt confident the economic recovery had legs, Baker and I recommended that the president begin explicitly taking credit for the improving economy. Only through constant repetition of the same message, we advised, would the public make the connection between President Reagan's leadership and their lives.

But taking credit for things was never his strong suit. It was his greatest communicative weakness, if one can call it that. I honestly believe his self-effacing personality often accounted for his opponents' attacks on his intelligence. He was always quick to diminish himself in order to lift others up.

In the wake of the president's passing, Fox News's national political reporter Chris Wallace reminded me of a story from the 1980 presidential campaign that illustrates this point. Wallace and I were traveling together on Reagan's campaign plane a few weeks before the election, and he asked me to explain our strategy for winning the requisite number of electoral votes needed to gain the White House. I took out a scratch piece of paper, drew a map of the United States, and began filling the page with how I believed the electoral vote would divide. Wallace kept the paper.

Following Reagan's landslide victory, Wallace took the little map I had drawn and showed it to the president. The reporter then asked Reagan if he wouldn't mind signing it as a memento. Reagan took the map, thought for a second, flashed that little wry smile that he so often did, and scribbled something on the page before handing it back to him. Wallace looked down at the paper and saw that it read, "I don't understand what this means. Ronald Reagan."

Reagan's critics probably thought he was being literal. But anyone who knew him well would tell you that the president often used self-deprecating humor as a way of sharing credit with others. He didn't feel the need to steal others' spotlight. He'd been in the spotlight all his life. One of the things that made Reagan effective as a communicator was that audiences sensed he was comfortable in his own skin. They sensed that he didn't feel the need to act like someone else. Indeed, there was a natural gracefulness about the way he interacted with others that was hard to define.

One day during the first week of June I arrived at the Oval Office about fifteen minutes early for my 4 p.m. meeting with the president. I asked Reagan's secretary whether the projector and screen were set up for my slide presentation. She said that they were, but added that if I wanted to go check on them I could. So I went into the Oval Office and began fiddling with the equipment. Suddenly I stopped and sort of froze for a second before looking up. It was the first time I had ever been alone in the Oval Office.

It's an odd feeling, standing alone at the epicenter of world power. I honestly don't know how the cleaning staff does their job without getting goose bumps. I don't care how many years you've been in presidential politics or how many presidents you've worked for, you never lose that sense of awe and grandeur when entering the Oval Office. I know Ronald Reagan sure didn't. Mike Deaver once suggested to him that he might take off his suit jacket to make himself more comfortable when working alone in the Oval Office. President Reagan said he wouldn't dream of doing such a thing. He said he respected the office too much to ever remove his jacket.

Standing there alone in the Oval Office, I noticed that President Reagan was outside on the lawn attending a function. I decided to walk out to meet him. Along the way, I met up with Baker. As we walked outside past the Rose Garden, Jim asked whether I could see where the president was. "Yes, I see him coming now," I replied.

There was a Marine band on a podium out on the South Lawn playing to a relatively small crowd. But as I watched Reagan walk through the crowd shaking hands and recognizing virtually anyone who approached him, I was reminded of a fly-fishing trip I had taken in Pennsylvania with master fly fisherman Frank Johnson. Reagan gave the nod, the recognition, the hand-shake with the same deft skill I had seen Johnson use when floating the fly at the end of his fishing line out over the water before making it gently kiss the surface. Filled with grace and ease, both men were confident and skilled in their abilities.

And Reagan would need these communicative abilities, because despite the improvements in the economy, in the latter part of 1983 a series of foreign policy crises threatened to shake Americans' confidence in their president's ability to lead.

The first of these happened on September 1, 1983, when the Soviets downed Korean Air Lines flight 007. Once it had been confirmed that the plane was, in fact, shot down, I called Ed Meese and told him that I felt it was very important to have the president out in front on the issue. I wanted Reagan to speak to the nation immediately in order to calm concerns. The situation was complicated by the fact that the president was on vacation at the time. Having the image of the KAL 007 massacre playing against footage of the president out horseback riding would send the American people the wrong message. Ed promised me he would relay the message. I then spoke with Jim Baker and repeated my concerns. Jim said, "You wouldn't want the president coming home in a panic, would you?"

"No," I replied, "that would send the wrong signal. But we do have to get him in this news cycle."

After I got off the phone with Baker, Stu Spencer called. He asked for my thoughts about the crisis. As I was relaying the same message I had told Meese and Baker, I flipped on the television only to find CBS News doing exactly as I had feared. They were showing a simulated crash of the plane that cut directly to a picture of Reagan riding on horseback.

Reagan had apparently made up his mind not to issue a statement. Stu said he had called and tried to get the president to budge from his earlier position. He said he thought he had moved the president a little, but asked that I place a follow-up call at his and Nancy's request, which I did.

The president sounded very somber and serious on the tele-

phone, but, as always, his voice was cheerful and warm. I apologized for interrupting his vacation but told him the circumstances were extremely serious. I then told him that I thought
it was very important for him to go down, hold a short press
conference, not take any questions, go up the stairs to the
entrance of Air Force One, and fly back to Washington.

President Reagan said he thought that would be a good idea
before adding, "But I think there is a better way to avoid taking questions. I'll take one question and then, Dick, as you
have suggested, I'll say that I'm going back to Washington to
determine what the facts of the case are and what our response
to those facts will be." I told him that would work well and
wished him the best of luck.

But Reagan would need much more than luck to manage
the next series of foreign policy crises he would soon face
involving Lebanon and Grenada. On October 23, 1983, 214
U.S. Marines were murdered in a surprise suicide bombing
attack on our barracks in Beirut, Lebanon. Reagan's secretary
of defense, Caspar Weinberger, had warned of the danger in
keeping the troops there on the ground. But Cap's protesta-
tions had gone unheeded. Reagan grieved the loss of American
life deeply, and he took the blame squarely upon himself. With
Americans mourning the murder of our Marines in Beirut, the
president's support was in danger of being seriously fractured.

But in the wake of the nation's grief over Lebanon, another
foreign policy crisis erupted almost immediately elsewhere in
the world. This incident would force Reagan to take action in
the small Caribbean island of Grenada. Under threat of a possible Marxist takeover, a group of American students at the St.
George's School of Medicine in Grenada had been placed in
harm's way. The plan to invade Grenada had been under way
before the massacre in Lebanon had ever occurred. Indeed, it
is a testament to President Reagan's resolve that in the wake of
the horrible events in Lebanon, he stayed the course in
Grenada. And yet Reagan's political opponents hadn't seen it

that way. His critics thought Grenada was little more than a diversion from what they considered his questionable judgment in Lebanon. But while the two were related, one had not caused the other.

The president needed to regain control of the situation and reassure the American people, and he needed to do it quickly. In a matter of days, two major military events—one in Lebanon and the other in Grenada—had taken place. Just as with the KAL 007 tragedy, my impulse was to put Reagan in front of the American people. Indeed, after some high-level discussions, the president decided he would deliver a prime-time televised address on October 27, 1983, wherein he would discuss the downing of the KAL 007, as well as the events in Lebanon and Grenada. The speech produced one of the most dramatic changes in public opinion I ever recorded in all my years with Reagan.

My research indicated that nearly two-thirds (64 percent) of the adult population either saw, heard, or read the president's speech to the nation. Positive reactions to the speech outweighed negative reactions by a massive three-to-one ratio (71 percent favorable, 24 percent unfavorable). By responding quickly to inform the nation of his policies and purposes in both Lebanon and Grenada, Reagan effectively reversed the immediate erosion of public support for his conduct of American foreign policy generally, and his handling of the situations in Lebanon and Grenada specifically.

The day before the speech, only 43 percent of the nation said they approved of Reagan's handling of foreign affairs. After his speech, however, that number soared to 58 percent. As for his handling of Grenada, prior to the speech only 44 percent had indicated support. After the speech the number stood at 64 percent—a twenty-point increase in positive public attitudes. Reagan's address was further evidence of his ability to employ his powers of persuasion in order to lead during times of crisis.

With few exceptions, my counsel to Ronald Reagan was almost always the same: take your case directly to the American people. I was supremely confident in the Greatest Communicator's ability to project calm in the face of uncertainty. I had seen him do it dozens of times, going back to our days in California. From a strategic perspective, when facing a challenge I felt the answer was almost always to have Ronald Reagan speak. It was like putting the ball in the hands of your star player with the score tied and ten seconds left in the game. You could always count on him to produce in the clutch.

Toward the end of 1983, and with the 1984 presidential election just over the horizon, Ronald Reagan still hadn't officially declared his intention to run for reelection. He always liked to hold out until the last possible moment. Still, despite his age, we all suspected he would run.

Around this time, Jim Baker and I met with the president in the Oval Office. I pointed out that the key to 1984 would be the extent to which the vision we created in 1980 would, in fact, be something we could show had been realized.

I then spoke in personal terms. I told the president that my son, John, was four years old, and that the theme of the reelection campaign, should it be launched, should really focus on John, not as a four-year-old, but as a twenty-four-year-old. I challenged Reagan to continue thinking not only about what the opportunities for positive change might be in 1988, but what they might be through the years 2000 and 2004 when John would be grown up.

Reagan sat in rapt attention. My intimate tone resonated with him, just as I had hoped it might.

I was merely reflecting what I had seen my mentor—Reagan—do for so many years: use a personal story to illustrate a point. He had taught me so much just by letting me learn through his example.

With the 1984 election staring us in the face, I was eager to ensure that America—indeed, the world—would have another four years to benefit from the president's leadership.

As Baker and I stood up to end our meeting, I looked Reagan in the eye and said, "Mr. President, Jim Baker, myself, and others are beginning to put together the plans for your 1984 campaign. How do you feel about that?"

Reagan looked at me, winked, smiled and said, "Dick, you just keep on planning."

5

"You Ain't Seen Nothin' Yet!"

The 1984 Landslide

America's best days are yet to come. And I know it
may drive my opponents up the wall, but I'm going to
say it anyway—you ain't seen nothin' yet.
— Ronald Reagan, campaign rally, Fairfield, Connecticut,
October 26, 1984

On May 15, 1984, President Reagan and I had been visiting in the Oval Office.

"Hey, Dick," said the president, "have you heard the one about the old man and his friend?"

"No, Mr. President, I haven't."

"Well, on one particular afternoon, an old man and his friend had been visiting with one another. The friend said to the old man, 'I bet I can tell you exactly how old you are.'

"The old man replied, 'How can you do that?'

"'Easily,' said the friend. 'First turn around.' The old man turned around.

"'Second, pull down your pants.' The old man pulled down his pants.

"'Now pull down your shorts,' and the old man pulled down his shorts.

"And then he said to the old man, 'All right, pull up your shorts'—which the old man did.

"'Now pull up your pants,' and the old man pulled up his pants.

"Then the friend said, 'Now turn around,' and the old man turned around.

"The friend looked the old man right in the eye and said, 'You're ninety-four years, five months, and three days.'

"The old man was astounded. 'How could you ever guess precisely how old I am?' he asked.

"The friend paused, then said, 'Because you told me yesterday.'"

As you might imagine, Reagan and I laughed a good while. The president said Bob Hope had told him the joke. But embedded in the punch line was an essential, if unfortunate, political truth: given voters' often limited political memories (the old man), savvy opponents can sometimes get voters to make bad choices by offering distracting information (the friend).

As we entered the 1984 presidential election season, some in our camp were signaling they believed Reagan should focus only on his past achievements instead of talking about his vision for the future. To be fair, given the success of Reagan's first term, I understood their initial impulse. President Reagan had taken America from a time of malaise to one of optimism and hope. Indeed, by election day, the economy would be booming, interest rates would be falling, and the American military would be getting stronger. In sum, times were good and getting better. Without question, these successes would be an integral part of our campaign.

But after studying mountains of data and having run dozens of campaigns, I was convinced that the president's overarching campaign theme should take a decidedly "future" focus. While our message should meet the challenges of the last four years, I felt that the 1984 theme must focus on the future. But most of all, I knew that Reagan believed that elections are always about the future. As he would say hundreds of times in 1984 from the stump, "America's best days are yet to come. . . . You ain't seen nothin' yet!"

The conventional political wisdom holds that presidential elections are always a referendum on an incumbent president's first term. This is in part true. But one of the biggest traps presidents seeking a second term can fall into is to communicate solely about the past. By forcing an incumbent president to stare in the rearview mirror constantly, an opponent may invite voters to question the president's ability to provide forward-looking leadership. And that's what I feared some on our campaign team were prepared to do. They were approaching the 1984 election with a 1980 mentality. But Reagan was no longer a challenger. He was an incumbent, and there is a big difference between the two.

When President Reagan had told me to "just keep on planning," I was determined that we avoid applying a "one size fits all" approach to the 1984 campaign. As the incumbent, Ronald Reagan would face a new set of political realities. While it is true that incumbency provides presidents with opportunities, it comes with obstacles as well.

On the plus side, incumbent presidents can control, at least more effectively than anyone else in America, the timing of key governmental actions, policies, and announcements, thus directly influencing the national agenda at any given time. Also, in times of international stability, the incumbent president is often credited with the improved state of the world regardless of whether credit is truly deserved. Finally, an incumbent running for reelection gets double media coverage—he is both president and presidential contender.

But these positives are not without their corollaries. First, in foreign affairs he will be held responsible for international crises not of his own doing. Second, his record over the last four years will become a target for those who aspire to replace him. And lastly, while he will enjoy double coverage as president and candidate when the news is favorable, so also will he be hit twice when the news is bad. Given the media's propensity toward conflict and negative news, more time in the spotlight isn't always a good thing. In sum, while Ronald Reagan's status as an incumbent would bring both advantages and disadvantages, my goal was to maximize the former and minimize the latter.

So in October 1983 I produced what became the sequel to the Black Book—the 1984 Reagan Campaign Action Plan, a document that ran some 180 pages in length. After having the plan in his possession a few days, Reagan joked that, due to the secretive nature of it all, he didn't know whether he should hand the campaign book plan over to the Secret Service. Mike Deaver quipped, "You don't need to do that, Mr. President. Just tuck it under your pillow at night."

As with the Black Book, the 1984 Campaign Action Plan outlined strategic objectives, suggested a thematic frame of reference for the upcoming election, blocked out a series of action steps, assessed the strengths and weaknesses of our prospective Democratic opponents, and began doing the detailed and critical work of studying the internal dynamics of key battleground states, states that could decide the outcome of the race. If I had to give all presidential candidates and strategists one piece of advice, it would be to focus on this last element. National campaigns are won and lost in the details. Moreover, presidential elections are actually fifty separate elections. It's a simple truth, but one that is easily forgotten.

So with that truth in mind, I set out upon the task of crafting Reagan's 1984 campaign plan. Here is the first paragraph of that document:

Political campaign plans should neither be chiseled in granite nor written in sand. Plans must change with the inevitable fluctuation of the pace, scope, and thrust of the political contest. Contrarily, without well-defined and stable objectives, the scarce resources of a presidential campaign are quickly squandered. Hence, this document establishes objectives and initiates a continuing process of planning that will cease only after November 6, 1984. Such planning does not deal with future decisions, but with the future of present decisions.

One advantage we had working in our favor was the edge that incumbent presidents historically enjoy over challengers. Still, we were quick to remind ourselves that just four years ago a governor from California named Ronald Reagan had bucked that trend by running a highly organized and disciplined campaign. So the Campaign Action Plan cautioned that "we can only assume (in spite of some strong political assets) that we face a very tough challenge in 1984."

I was reflecting my own approach to political planning and the president's as well. If there was one thing Ronald Reagan despised it was hubris, particularly in the midst of an election. He believed you should always run a campaign as if you were ten points behind. "We can't take anything for granted," he would say. And that meant being prepared to run against any eventual Democratic challenger.

I like to think of politics as two-handed poker. Whether or not you win is determined not only by the cards you hold, but by your opponent's hand and how well you read his or her strategy. We had no way to know for sure whom the Democrats would select as their presidential nominee. So the campaign plan analyzed the political assets and liabilities of all the most likely Democratic candidates. We considered two candidates to be the front-runners of the Democratic field. Indeed, one of these two men concerned us much more than the other, and his name wasn't Walter Mondale.

As President Carter's former vice president, Walter Mondale seemed to be the odds-on favorite to win the Democratic nomination. He had strong name recognition and was well liked within the Democratic Party. We saw Mondale as a younger incarnation of his political mentor, Hubert Humphrey. That is to say, he was an unabashed, unadorned, liberal Democrat. Interestingly, Mondale said he believed Ronald Reagan would be the easiest Republican to beat because of his conservative record. We were eager to test his theory. While we considered Mondale a tough competitor, we knew he would face one major dilemma: how to distance himself from the unpopular Carter administration while at the same time remaining loyal to it.

This was a limitation not shared by the other Democratic front-runner at the time, the one we initially considered the greater threat, Senator John Glenn. Glenn possessed three formidable political assets that made him stronger than Mondale. First, he was the closest thing to a national hero American politics had seen in thirty years. He had five Distinguished Flying Crosses, an air medal with eighteen clusters for his service during World War II and Korea, the National Space Medal of Honor, the NASA Distinguished Service Medal, and he was the first American to orbit the earth. Second, he was well-known and well liked. Honestly, what wasn't there to like about a man who had so nobly served his country? And finally, my studies showed that Glenn was viewed as nonpartisan. In fact, Senator Glenn was as highly respected among conservative Republicans as he was among liberal Democrats.

These three advantages gave Glenn the potential to cut deeply into Reagan's base support and also to appeal to independent voters. When I studied voters' ideological perceptions of Glenn, I found he was viewed more warmly among the very conservative voters than he was among the very liberal! But as

Glenn's campaign rolled on, he made a series of gaffes that revealed his campaign skills to be not up to the standard of his prior service to his country.

One person who wasn't an ineffective campaigner, however, was dark-horse candidate Gary Hart, who had surged to the front of the Democratic pack. The Reagan campaign, like most political observers, hadn't anticipated that Hart would become a strong contender. But as his political star started to soar, I quickly began studying him much more closely. Toward the end of March, I ran two hypothetical ballots. The first was a matchup between Ronald Reagan and Walter Mondale. Among registered voters, Reagan trounced Mondale by twenty points. However, when the president was matched up against Gary Hart, Reagan's lead was cut to four points.

By the end of July, it was clear that with the Democratic National Convention just over the horizon, Reagan needed to begin driving home his three key strengths: economic growth, his trustworthiness, and strong leadership. While these three factors were beginning to trend in President Reagan's favor, I thought it important to urge the president not to be fooled by the polls that showed him beating Mondale soundly. My most recent data wasn't looking good. The time seemed right to give Reagan and my enthusiasm a gut check.

Upon entering the Oval Office and greeting the president one day, I noticed he was wearing a gold pin on his lapel. It almost looked like abstract jewelry. Upon closer examination, however, you could see that it was actually the rear end of a horse. When I commented on it, he said a friend of his who owned a gold mine in Montana had had it made for him to remind us all of what we may become if we don't make wise decisions. I told him that the pin reminded me of a comment my father, who used to run ranches, had made to me as a boy. Dad had said that before you buy a horse you ought to examine it carefully, both front end and back. I then told the president that the news I was going to give him was a little bit like his pin; it would start with the bad news first.

I explained that there was now measurably less enthusiasm about the economic recovery and that the race between himself and Mondale was beginning to tighten up, with Mondale just eight points behind. Also, earlier that morning, the president had given an impromptu press conference in which he had made an appeal for funding the MX missile. I told him that whenever he talked about "throw weights" and "megatonnage" it created a lot of concern. Then I reluctantly shared a statistic I knew he wouldn't want to hear.

"Mr. President," I said, "almost four out of ten Americans believe that a nuclear holocaust will annihilate mankind *in their lifetime.*"

A steely silence fell over the room. Given what he had shared with me privately in the White House residence about the legacy he had hoped to leave, I understood why.

"I know this has been a more pessimistic assessment than what you have been hearing from other quarters, but I felt that we should look at both the front end and the rear end of the horse," I said.

"I agree, Dick," said the president. "Understanding what's at the rear end of the horse is important, because that's where the power lies."

Having loved his phrasing and the meaning behind it—that you have to face undesirable news head-on in order to stay strong—I nodded in agreement.

"But in summary, what you're telling me, Dick, is that I'm doing everything wrong but that the people still support me?" he asked.

"No, Mr. President, I guess the summary would be that there is some concern, especially about foreign policy and the slowdown in the economy. But people who are still supporting your domestic policies, have some questions about your foreign policies, and yet still like you as an individual enough to support your presidency at this point."

Reagan's question to me about how voters could disagree with some of his policy positions and still stand solidly behind him is one that even today continues to confound many presidential scholars. In some ways, I'm not sure even Ronald Reagan fully grasped what it was about his rhetoric that made his words resonate so strongly with citizens, or why he was able to transcend policy differences while winning people's support. Part of the answer rested with the three strengths—trustworthiness, strong leadership, and accomplishing targeted objectives—he possessed, qualities we would showcase during the 1984 presidential campaign. But by themselves, those traits alone do not explain the "secret" behind Reagan's ability to conjure up such deep feelings of affection and admiration in the hearts and minds of so many Americans. So what does?

Now, in the wake of his passing, some of Reagan's detractors were confounded when hundreds of thousands of Americans formed lines that extended in some cases more than a mile in length and stood waiting for over eight hours just to see his casket.

Why did they do this? What was it about the Greatest Communicator that made people love him so?

After conducting hundreds of studies on President Reagan's leadership, and after having spent a quarter century at his side analyzing his every communicative move, I believe I can answer that question in that one word I raised earlier in talking about his communicative strength: values.

The reason Ronald Reagan continues to engender such a deep emotional response is that he communicated universally these shared values. While issues change, values endure. I defined values earlier as those beliefs that give life its meaning and worth. They are the "anchors" that order the world around us. We don't often think in terms of our values, but that is precisely why they wield such power. Like gravity, these invisible forces order the way we live, the choices we make, and the things we hold dear. Values are unchanging, transcendent, timeless. Politicians who speak about "issues" come and go. But that rare breed of leader whose rhetoric embodies broadly shared values in the context of issues represents an individual who will likely stand the test of time.

This fundamental truth of communicative leadership goes a long way toward explaining the depth of commitment and passion people feel when they talk about Ronald Reagan. I once told a reporter I would walk over hot coals for Reagan. Okay, so maybe that was a tad overstated, but the fact is Reagan struck powerful chords when he spoke. And it wasn't just with me. Listen to the language people use when talking about his legacy. I mean, honestly, can you imagine anyone referring to the Johnson Revolution, the Nixon Revolution, the Ford Revolution, the Carter Revolution, or the Clinton Revolution?

Me neither.

But the *Reagan* Revolution?

It fits.

"The Gipper" made you *want* to join his revolution. You knew his fight wasn't about himself. How could it be? This was a man who wanted to share credit at every turn. President Reagan was a leader who relished the fight because all would enjoy the prize. In fact, in private settings, he would become uncomfortable when conversation was concentrated solely on him. It was almost as if he had an internal seismograph, a monitor that could detect the slightest movement in focus toward himself. If it was triggered, he would shift concern away from himself and onto others.

I knew this move well. One time while we were meeting in the Oval Office, Reagan was wearing one of his favorite dark brown suits and looked well rested, but I remember noticing that he had a small patch on his nose covering an incision from a recent surgery. The doctors had closed the wound with blue stitches. When I asked him about the procedure, he quipped, "Well, I just wish the doctors would have given me something that was a little better color coordinated." After only a few minutes discussing his surgery, Reagan's seismograph had begun detecting the subtle tremors of conversational imbalance.

As we sat down, he decided to shift attention away from himself by asking me about the dark glasses I wore that day. I had broken a blood vessel, likely by lifting something a little too heavy on the weekend, and my whole eye was blood red. Like an attending physician, he asked me to come closer so he could examine it himself. After looking me over he said, "You know, Dick, that happens to me sometimes. Even though it doesn't hurt, I've found that Visine helps. I really think you should try some and see if that doesn't clear it up."

Here was the leader of the free world taking the time to offer advice on eye care. It was a deft example of Ronald Reagan simply being Ronald Reagan. His ability to shift attention from himself and onto someone else was so fluid, so seamless. And even though I'd seen him do it hundreds of times, if you weren't careful, you could miss it.

What Reagan taught me is that leaders who communicate their values while transferring attention away from themselves speak volumes. Doing so projects an image of self-assurance and concern for others. What could be more confident than implicitly saying, "I'm secure enough with myself that I don't feel the need to monopolize the spotlight"? In so doing, the president was engaged in a form of communicative sacrifice, a trait that would serve him well in his upcoming showdown with the eventual Democratic nominee for president of the United States.

That man's name was, of course, Walter Mondale. In the end, Jimmy Carter's former vice president would knock Hart out of the race just as he had John Glenn. Although he sustained several wounds in the process, Mondale emerged victorious from the Democratic primary season and nomination process and now enjoyed a substantial post-convention bounce. The twenty-point lead Reagan once held over Mondale had been cut by more than half.

As a result, the Reagan campaign team had begun shifting into high gear. Lee Atwater, Jim Baker, Mike Deaver, Ed Meese, Paul Laxalt, Lyn Nofziger, Ed Rollins, Stu Spencer, Bob Teeter, and I represented the cast of characters responsible for helping Ronald Reagan win reelection.

Three people who do not appear on that list but who were nonetheless an integral part of developing an important component of Reagan's strategy were Professor Tom Reynolds, John Moss, and John Fiedler. These individuals helped me devise a quantitative instrument that, like PINS before it, would help Reagan chart a course to presidential victory. Reynolds dubbed the new tool a Hierarchical Values Map (HVM).

As I discussed earlier, Ronald Reagan's rhetoric spun on the axis of values. After years of analyzing this dimension of Reagan's communication, I began researching the scholarly literature on how values influence human behavior and, more specifically, the attitudes people hold. Tom Reynolds, a leading scholar on the issue, devised a theoretical model capable of mapping voters' decisions based on three factors: issues, policy program traits, and values. The HVM itself looked like a spiderweb with rectangles sprinkled throughout. It allowed me to monitor which candidate, Mondale or Reagan, "owned" which issues and which values, and to understand the linkages between them. For example, in August of 1984, Mondale owned the rectangles that led to the value of "Security for Oneself/Children's Future."

Given that finding, three imperatives were developed that would later help to guide President Reagan's television advertising strategy. First, our television ads would need to challenge the fairness of Mondale's proposed tax increase. Second, we would need to connect the need to strengthen national defense with the preservation of world peace. And finally, the HVM suggested we must continue reinforcing the president's image as a strong, effective leader.

With map in hand, we set out to create a series of television advertisements that would neutralize Walter Mondale's "lock" on the "Security for Oneself/Children's Future" rectangle. To do this, we would be joined by the team tasked with creating President Reagan's campaign television commercials. These individuals became known as the "Tuesday Team," a name that derived from the first Tuesday following the election in November. The Tuesday Team was composed of some of Madison Avenue's top advertising wizards. Phil Dusenberry, one of the most talented ad men in the business, headed the advisory committee overseeing all creative work for the campaign. During one of their meetings, Reagan surprised members when he peeked his head in the door. "I understand you're all here selling soap," he said. "So I thought you'd like to see the bar." A candidate who was confident enough to call himself a product? The admen loved it.

Once the Tuesday Team produced the spots, I would then test them to gauge audience reactions. To achieve the HVM's first imperative—challenging the fairness of Mondale's plan to raise taxes—the team had created a thirty-second spot that asked the question, "Are you willing to work harder to pay for Walter Mondale's campaign promises?" It scored well.

But the second ad, and one of Ronald Reagan's personal favorites, is now among the most famous pieces of campaign advertising ever created. We called it the "Bear Ad." This thirty-second spot was designed to achieve the HVM's second imperative—stress Reagan's theme of achieving peace and a sense of security through strength. The ad presented viewers with a parable about a bear. (Parables have seldom been used in campaigns before or since this one.) The visual was of a grizzly bear lumbering through the woods and across a field set to the following script: "There is a bear in the woods. For some people the bear is easy to see. Others don't see it at all. Some people say the bear is tame. Others say it's vicious and dangerous. Since no one can really be sure who's right, isn't it smart to be as strong as the bear? If there is a bear."

Test audiences went wild; they loved it. Viewer recall rates were remarkably high (68 percent). The number of individuals who remembered the central message of the ad was exceedingly high as well (56 percent). Most importantly, people understood the central message: strength is the best way to achieve peace. In the executive summary of my memorandum about the Bear Ad I wrote, "In conclusion, the 'Bear' ad proved itself to have the potential of being one of the most effective and memorable ads to come along for a long time . . . the ad should be used frequently."

However, the most important pre-test of all happened when we showed the spot to President Reagan to get his final approval. After the tape was finished rolling, Reagan said, "I like that one!" So much so that he wanted to show it to certain congressmen on the Hill.

I am often asked about another advertising sally from that campaign, a series of spots we ran early in the spring of 1984, the so-called Morning in America ads. These spots represented one of our single biggest expenditures of the entire campaign. You may recall that these were the beautifully executed ads that highlighted optimism and hope, all packed under the tagline "Morning in America." Well, just like the myth about Reagan's line in the Nashua debate—"I paid for this microphone"—being the decisive event that won that election, so too is it a myth that these ads triggered the November landslide. They did not. In spite of the tremendous resources spent during that media blitz, in point of fact, these spots did not move the president's vote support at all. However, they provided a positive and upbeat context for voters.

But, it was only when the campaign messages centered on

the president's leadership strengths, his vision for America, and his accomplishments that a compelling rationale for a Reagan vote began to shift slowly and then decisively in favor of the incumbent president.

With just sixty-two days to go until the election, and with the conventions now behind us, the president, Nancy, Jim Baker, and I found ourselves thousands of feet above the earth, soaring along aboard Air Force One. There probably isn't any plane like it in the world. It was designed almost exclusively for the comfort and the communications convenience of the president of the United States. The front half of the aircraft contained a communications center manned by three Air Force radio operators. Then came the galley, the president's office, lounge, and the mini conference area, which included three or four tables for staff along with two secretarial stations. Beyond that point there was room for approximately thirty passengers.

Through the years I always found the service and food on Air Force One to be excellent. Although I had worked previously for Presidents Nixon and Ford, because all of my flights aboard Air Force One were during Reagan's two terms, I don't know if it was always customary to put as much candy on the plane as they did for the Reagans. From 1980 to 1988, Air Force One was like a candy store with wings. And it wasn't just jelly beans. They had that plane stocked with virtually every goody that might appeal to the sweet tooth. There was some form of candy on virtually every table, and in some of the nooks and crannies as well.

I guess the only thing I didn't like about Air Force One was the color of the decor, which, back then anyway, was a light turquoise blue. For some reason it always reminded me of a cheap 1960s motel.

On this particular trip, the president and Nancy sat in front of me at the stateroom table, with Reagan to my right and

Nancy to my left. I sat in the middle of the couch, with Jim Baker on my right.

Presenting data on Air Force One was always a bit awkward because of the sound levels. Physically, the stateroom was built primarily for study, less for conferencing, and clearly not to review data. As I started my presentation, Nancy got up and turned off all the air vents to reduce the noise level.

That day's presentation was an important one. I began by telling Nancy and the president that while the hot sun, dusty motorcade, crush of the crowds, and hectic schedules were all part of the business of running for election, it was also a great adventure that we all knew would last only sixty-two days longer. I pointed out that we were starting the race from a better initial position than any contest I had chronicled for the president.

Jim interjected that Walter Mondale had been attacking Reagan very personally that day, hurling the tired old mantra that Democrats had repeated for years; namely, that the president favored only the "country club" set rather than all Americans. Both Jim and I told Reagan that these were the kinds of charges he could expect over the next forty days. However, I said that they did not in any way require a response.

Always disliking to be attacked, the president said, "I've never even belonged to a country club!"

As we reviewed the numbers, I showed the president the strong boost he had received from our convention in Dallas. Reagan had entered the Republican National Convention with an eight-point lead. He emerged with a sixteen-point advantage. I was most encouraged to see that more of the electorate felt the president would deal with future problems boldly and aggressively. Our renewed emphasis on a future-oriented theme had helped us on that question considerably.

I concluded by telling the president we might have a chance to "McGovernize" Mondale—that is, set up a circumstance wherein he was simply not taken seriously as a presidential candidate by showing that his campaign had become one of desperation and deceit. We agreed to meet after my next study was complete.

A few weeks after our trip aboard Air Force One, Jim Baker and I met with the president in the Oval Office and were joined briefly by Secretary of State George Schultz. Despite a strenuous campaign tour in Iowa, Reagan looked well rested. I told the president that he enjoyed a massive lead that, if it held, would give us a win on the dimensions of the Roosevelt-Johnson-Nixon landslides—the three largest presidential victories of the last century. But I warned that it all hinged on a big "if." And that if was whether we could hold on to the "Reagan Democrats" as well as independent and younger voters. I also reiterated that we needed to continue combating the Democratic distortion that the Reagan administration was unfair, uncaring, and likely to start an unnecessary war.

"While Mondale is talking a lot," I told the president, "no one is really listening to him. If you take him on point-by-point, Mr. President, all we will end up doing is enhancing his credibility."

"Yes, but just the other night, Dick, I saw one of their ads saying how we had hurt the old and the elderly and were unfair, and so on. The thing is, even water dripping on a rock can eventually wear it down," Reagan said.

"Well, Mr. President that is very true. But, as my mother used to say, 'Patience is a virtue. There is a time and a season for all things.' You will have an opportunity to take Mondale on directly and confront him in the debates. If Mondale's ads begin to penetrate your support, we will definitely counter with ads of our own. Just to underscore what I'm saying, though, about no one listening to Mondale, I thought you'd appreciate this."

I then reached across and handed the president a cartoon that showed Mondale being caricatured as Chicken Little with the caption, "The Sky Is Falling!"

He laughed.

Baker then offered the president a Velamint. Baker loved those things—he would often eat one after another during meetings. That company's stock must have risen and fallen with Jim's travel schedule. Anyhow, the president hesitated before accepting the mint and popping it in his mouth. I had just been talking about how Americans viewed him as decisive compared to Mondale. Seeing Reagan hesitate before taking the breath mint, Jim said, "I don't know, Dick. Maybe the president isn't as decisive as you think." We all smiled. But then the president got serious.

Reagan told us that just moments before our meeting he had had a phone conversation with the mother of an American serviceman who had lost his life during the recent bombing attack in Lebanon. The president always maintained that sending troops into harm's way was a commander in chief's most gut-wrenching duty. Yet even though consoling the bereaved was always hard, Reagan felt a solemn responsibility and desire to support the families of our fallen heroes any way he could.

President Reagan said that the soldier's mother was, of course, extremely upset. But through the tears and sobbing she explained that her son had strong beliefs in what we were trying to do in Lebanon and that he had faith in Reagan as commander in chief. She went on to say that she had been getting incessant calls from reporters who wanted her to renounce the president's leadership or to offer bitter comments. Toward the end of the conversation, she began to get choked up, so much so, in fact, that President Reagan said it was almost impossible to understand her. Hearing his sister's uncontrollable sobbing, the woman's brother snatched the phone out of her hand. In a loud and angry voice he yelled, "WHO IS THIS?!"

At this point in Reagan's story, Baker and I exchanged glances, glances that said, *Where is he going with this? Please, please, please tell me this story isn't going to end up on the front page of tomorrow's* Washington Post.

"So," Reagan continued, "I just told him my name. I said, 'Ronald Reagan.'"

Can you imagine being the man on the other end of the phone?

The amount of adrenaline that must have surged through that young man's body could have probably powered New York City for a day.

After a moment of stunned silence, Reagan said the man started apologizing profusely for yelling at the president of the United States. He said he was terribly embarrassed. While showering the president with a deluge of "Mr. President, I am *so* very sorry" statements, the brother explained that the media's incessant harassment had the whole family in knots.

Reagan calmed the young man down. He told him not to worry about his mistake. The president said he understood completely; reporters can have that effect on people. He didn't think twice about the man's mistake. All he cared about was that mother's pain.

As should be clear by now, to Reagan the presidency wasn't about an individual. It was a stewardship, a way of serving others. I don't care if you were the wealthiest man alive or homeless, he treated you the same. He treated others with respect, and it showed in the way he spoke.

But for all his rhetorical prowess, Reagan did exhibit rare moments of oratorical uncertainty. Two of these happened during the 1984 presidential campaign.

The first had occurred out on the campaign trail when the candidate, not realizing there was a "hot" microphone in the vicinity, joked, "We'll begin bombing the Russians in five minutes." Some in the immediate audience laughed. The Russians weren't among them. It certainly didn't help Reagan's image on the so-called red button issue. But in the grand scheme of things it ended up being relatively negligible in terms of affecting voter attitudes. In fact, my tracking polls showed that

Reagan's lead over Mondale actually went up slightly in the wake of his comment.

But President Reagan's second rhetorical blunder stood to inflict much greater political harm. It happened during what became the big event of the 1984 presidential campaign: the presidential debates.

In 1984, President Reagan and former vice president Mondale agreed to participate in two presidential debates. The first of these was held on October 7 in Louisville, the second in Kansas City two weeks later.

Ronald Reagan's 1980 debate with Carter and his 1984 debates with Mondale were as different as they were similar. During both elections, Reagan prepared in advance by facing off with David Stockman as his debate partner, although, in my estimation, he had never needed to debate in the first place. Just as before, my data revealed that we were well positioned for victory, with Ronald Reagan pretty much wrapping up the election by October. On the day of the first debate my tracking polls had us with a twenty-point advantage. With only four weeks to go, it was an enormous lead.

Team Mondale was reading the same numbers, and that's what made them dangerous. They needed something *big* to happen. Roughly a week before the first debate, Patrick Caddell, President Carter's strategist and pollster, had sent the Mondale campaign a memorandum that argued among other things that the Democratic candidate was so far behind that the only way he would have a chance at winning would be to surprise Reagan with something entirely unexpected. So Mondale began sharpening his oratorical swords.

But while the Democrats were vigorously prepping their candidate, we were busy keeping Reagan away from the media and letting him get away with little to no practice. Initially a general consensus had formed that it would be less vital to bog the president down with a lot of needless detail. Why? Well, there were two reasons.

One was that Nancy seemed to want the president not to be overly consumed by the campaign process and, specifically, debate prep. She had seen her husband handle debate opponents all her life. You mustn't forget that by 1984 Ronald Reagan was a seasoned debater with several impressive wins under his belt, including the time he beat Bobby Kennedy in a debate when the two men went toe to toe. Although I can't say for certain, I suspect that, like the rest of us, she was confident her Ronnie was going to win reelection and didn't think it necessary for the commander in chief to expend what is any president's most precious resource—time—on a foregone conclusion.

And that sentiment reflects the second reason why less attention was given to debate preparations. When an incumbent president runs for reelection he becomes a rope stretched between two forces that often pull him in opposite directions: the campaign people and the White House people. The campaign people believe that the president must devote every waking minute to the cause of getting reelected. Without winning reelection, their argument goes, the White House people will be out of a job. The campaign people live by an old but true axiom: you can't save the world until you save your seat in government.

The White House people, on the other hand, don't always see it that way. They believe that the president has an obligation and duty to devote himself to matters of governance and policy regardless of the season. Just because it happens to be an election year doesn't mean the president stops being the president, the White House people contend. Their view is, if he leads responsibly, reelection will come.

It may seem counterproductive to those who have never been around the process, this business about tugging a president in two directions. And it is. But it's a reality that every incumbent president faces. Presidential challengers are often better prepared for debates than incumbents for a very simple reason: they don't have a country to run.

Once Reagan started his mock debates with Stockman it became clear that his time off had dulled his normally razor-sharp skills. Three days before the Louisville debates I remember sitting in the big, cold room we were using to prep the president. At one point Stockman had so frustrated Reagan on a point about Social Security that he actually yelled, "Shut up!" right in the middle of Stockman's statement.

And that's when we all started to get a little nervous. In terms of debate prep, we had let him off too easy. Maybe we were suffering from overconfidence; I'm not sure. But whatever it was, we had let our president down.

So we did the worst thing you can do to a candidate three days before a televised debate. We began cramming his head with all kinds of information. Reagan had never met a briefing book or strategy memo he didn't like. He would devour them, which normally would be fine. But not three days before a nationally televised debate! I think we had all become so accustomed to him rhetorically outfoxing his opponents that we all rationalized he would be okay against Fritz Mondale.

But voters were used to seeing the Greatest Communicator live up to his name. And in my view, that is the real story of Reagan's first debate against Mondale. Our campaign had failed to play and win the "expectations game." Going in, voters were expecting Ronald Reagan to wipe the floor with Mondale just as he had done against President Carter in 1980. "There you go again," and "Are you better off than you were four years ago?" were still fresh in voters' minds. They were expecting the smiling, witty soldier they knew and loved. What they got was something different.

The pivotal moment came during Reagan's closing statement when he seemed to ramble aimlessly about driving down the California coast. I remember it distinctly. I had set up a focus group to watch the debate live. The participants seemed surprised at President Reagan's lack of fluidity in answering some of the questions as well as when he went off on his tangent at the close of the debate. They had expected an impressive showing and were disappointed.

Immediately I knew that the president's performance was going to raise concern about an issue I had studied closely going all the way back to Reagan's first real run in 1976: his age. By this point he was seventy-three years old. His good looks and youthful spirit had always kept voters' concerns at bay, but not now. I knew his performance in Louisville would reopen the issue.

We all felt terribly responsible for the whole thing. By making him cram just hours before the debate, we had in effect short-circuited the president's greatest communicative asset—his instincts.

President Reagan once told a story about his days in show business that I think illustrates this point well.

Just off the Oval Office there is a small study. If you've ever been inside the White House, perhaps you've seen it. Anyhow, back then the room contained only two chairs and a television.

On May 15, 1984, crammed into that tiny space, six men—Mike Deaver, Senator Paul Laxalt, Jim Travis, Ed Rollins, President Reagan, and me—stood in a semicircle around the television.

We had assembled to view early cuts of possible commercials for the president's reelection campaign. After we spent several minutes staring at the color bars on the screen, it became clear that the White House technical crew was having difficulty loading the videotape. So Reagan did what he often did in situations like this. He told a story.

"Fellas, this sort of reminds me of when I used to work for *GE Theater*. At that time color television was just coming in and it took a complex and involved process of hand adjusting through mixers to get the color balance just right. Well, I remember one day someone said that a bunch of bananas that were part of the set appeared purple onscreen.

"Two hours before the program was to air, the director asked the color technicians how things were going. The answer came back that they were still having some problems.

"An hour later, the same question, the same answer. Thirty minutes before the program, and now near panic had broken out in the color department.

"Fifteen minutes to air and the director, now exasperated, said, 'Are we set?!'

"'Well,' the color technician responded, 'the bananas are now yellow, but all the people are green!'"

In addition to its being humorous, I've always felt there was an important communicative lesson just beneath its surface, a lesson that pertained directly to the error our team had made when prepping the president for his first debate against Walter Mondale. By focusing Reagan so intently on a batch of purple bananas (debate prep materials) just moments before show-time, we had turned our *candidate* green!

In an eerie foreshadowing of what was to come, the 1984 Campaign Action Plan had specifically addressed the tendency of news media to scrutinize a president's every action while simultaneously distilling "important" news into ninety-second sound bites that were often interlaced with cynical and negative editorial observations. When cataloguing some of the pitfalls of incumbency, I noted that these observations tend to focus "on failures rather than successes, on hope lost rather than hope gained, and erodes public patience and support for a sitting president. . . . In short, television is powerful, intimate, uncontrolled, and thereby, potentially damaging to an incumbent president."

For the next several days, Reagan's meandering debate statement became grist for the media mill. The Mondale campaign wasn't complaining. Neither were the political pundits and reporters who were hungry to spice up what had once appeared would be a Reagan cakewalk.

On October 10, I received a call around 9:20 a.m. from a deeply concerned Nancy Reagan. I had studies in the field and she knew they were slated to be back and tabulated soon. Nancy wanted the results firsthand and right away. Not surprisingly, my polls indicated that Mondale had indeed benefited from the president's mishaps in Louisville. Following the debate, the president's lead had been cut to twelve percentage points. Nancy said she wanted me to call President Reagan and go over the data with him.

Reagan and I spent about twenty minutes on the phone. He wasted no time in letting me know how he was feeling.

"Dick, I'm concerned. I know I didn't do well during the debate the other night, and I've got to tell you, it's been bothering me ever since."

"Well, Mr. President, I understand your concerns, but let me go over where we are to put it in perspective. As you might imagine, we have experienced some erosion since Louisville. As it stands, we lead by twelve points. But given Mondale's heavy ad buys and the negative attacks from the press, I think we should be fairly encouraged that we hold a lead of this size. Your job rating is showing 62 percent approval on the economy, and your three strongest assets are holding steady."

"That's good to hear, Dick."

"And, Mr. President, I want you to know that a lot of us think we all let you down in preparing you for the debate. We didn't serve you well."

"Well, I don't know about that. But I just had such a flurry of papers that I was trying to remember every fact that I possibly could."

"I know. I understand completely. But I still feel confident we are going to win this campaign."

"Dick, I wish we could visit longer, but I've got to get on

the helicopter here in three minutes. Thanks so much for getting my day started on this note," he replied.

When I hung up the phone I vowed the next debate in Kansas City would turn out differently. And I wasn't alone. In that period between Reagan's first and second debates we were all focused on one goal: preparing the president for rhetorical battle.

As I remember it, we all took slightly different approaches on how we would redeem ourselves after the first debate. Yet all our approaches took a similar thrust—helping him regain his confidence and forgive himself. That's the kind of man we were dealing with. He took responsibility for things that weren't his fault. Worse, he could be really hard on himself. During our phone conversation described above, I could feel the disappointment in his voice. I honestly think he was just as upset with himself as he was at the thought of somehow having let us down. It was all part of his deep desire to please others.

Someone once speculated that one of the reasons Reagan never let me leave his side all those years was that he viewed my data and analysis like a report card of himself. If his approval numbers were high, he could feel good that he was pleasing others. If they were low, he would sometimes get upset with himself and feel he had done something wrong. Some would say this trait was the predictable result of growing up with an alcoholic father. Whatever the reason, that was his way.

I remember the first time I comprehended this dimension of Ronald Reagan and the depth of what my numbers and analyses represented to him. It was during the first term and the president, Deaver, Meese, Baker, and I were meeting in the Oval Office. Everyone had anticipated that the news I brought that day wasn't good. Before I started, we had been sitting around swapping stories. And that's when I began to notice that there was sometimes a direct correlation between the number of stories the president would share and his level of concern about my findings. I realized that when Reagan was anxious about something I might tell him, he would begin spinning stories. He was trying to run out the clock. He had gone on for some time before Mike, ever the effective manager of the president's time, finally cut him off and said, "Mr. President, I think we better get started." With that, President Reagan braced himself for the voters' judgment. "Dick, what are the numbers?"

His was a curious blend of vulnerability and strength.

And too, I can't imagine that bearing the title of the Great Communicator made his loss in that first debate to Mondale any easier. Reagan's rhetorical acumen had become a part of his identity, something people expected of him. And again, he hated to disappoint.

Given all this, a general consensus formed that it was time to build our candidate up, let him know of our genuine confidence in his abilities, and get him in top shape for his next bout with Mondale. It was time to let Reagan be Reagan. Even though the president's numbers had already begun to stabilize and even tick back up before we arrived in Kansas City, with only two weeks left until election day, none of us were taking any chances. As is my nature, I began planning almost immediately. The first step involved drafting a memo for the president's eyes only.

The memorandum, dated October 12, was written just two days after my phone conversation with President Reagan. I began by outlining for the president his still sizable advantages over Mondale on the important areas of leadership and foreign affairs. For example, Reagan led Mondale by twenty-seven points on leadership qualities, thirteen points on his ability to deal with future problems, nine points on his ability to prepare the world for peace, and thirteen points on his ability to deal with problems in Central America. His only major deficit came on the question of which candidate was less likely to start an unnecessary war. Here, Mondale enjoyed a twenty-point advantage.

I then suggested that the president deal to his strengths of presidential leadership, the dramatic contrast between himself and Mondale, and his vision for the future. I encouraged him to speak from the experiences he had as president. "In the second debate, why not do what you do best?" I wrote. "One of your great resources is a wide range of presidential experiences." I then reminded him to do what he had taught me to do, that is, persuade through reason and motivate through emotion. "Think how the American people will feel about themselves and our country as you describe your thoughts, feelings, and visions for our future." Finally, I blocked out a series of issue areas and themes for him to review.

Shortly thereafter, we brought in Roger Ailes, the former media guru of several Republican campaigns, to assist in coaching our candidate. Roger had been a member of the Tuesday Group. Ailes is someone who understands the psychology involved in prepping a candidate for a live national television event, as well as the visual dynamics of television media. For instance, I've always been a fan of one of Roger's theories, something he calls the "Orchestra Pit Theory."

The theory says that a presidential candidate can deliver the most important speech of his entire life wherein he reveals the secret to achieving world peace, but if he happens to slip onstage and fall into the orchestra pit in the process, all reporters will focus on is that he fell into an orchestra pit, not that he revealed how to save the world. Thus, the Orchestra Pit Theory.

And that is why Reagan's miscue in Louisville had been so potentially damaging. Ailes and I agreed that the fundamental mistake of the first debate was placing the candidate in front of a tidal wave of information just three days before he was to do battle with Mondale. We decided to try something new.

Ailes and I met alone with the president. We told Reagan

we wanted to try a slightly different approach to preparing him for the debate. Roger said, "Mr. President, we are going to do a little batting practice. When we throw a question your way, all we want you to do is to follow your first instinct." We told him to "swing" naturally, stay on the offensive, and, whatever he did, not to overthink his response. Roger and I then began beaming question after question at him. Initially, he was still being too cautious in his responses; he was thinking too much. But then something wonderful happened. As we pelted him all types of pitches, the Reagan we had all grown accustomed to began breaking through the surface. We kept hurling harder and harder questions. And, one right after the other, he made contact, often cracking them out of the park.

Toward the end of the session, we had one final piece of business to address—the age issue. We told the president that the question of his age was likely to come up, either from one of the debate questioners or through a veiled reference from his opponent. We said we needed to think about how he might respond. That's when President Reagan looked at us, smiled, and said, "Don't you fellas worry about that. I'll handle that one."

The stage was set.

The location: Music Hall, Municipal Auditorium in Kansas City, Missouri.

The date: October 21, 1984.

After two weeks of negative news coverage and questions about the president's age, all eyes were on Ronald Reagan to see how he would perform. We had done everything we could. It was now time for our man to go out and deliver. We were a quirky bunch, us Reaganauts, and each of us had his own way of handling the anxiety that comes before an event like that. Some chose to watch the debate in their hotel rooms, others wrote Reagan little notes, and still others huddled together backstage around the television.

Me? I experienced Reagan's communicative event the way I

often did, by analyzing voters' responses in the form of a focus group. We set up a group of about forty voters in a hotel suite in Kansas City. Using an arcane version of a technology I would later modernize and implement consistently in the second term—more on that in the next chapter—viewers recorded their reactions to each candidate's performance using an electronic handheld dial that fed their responses into a tabulator.

While I enjoyed watching Reagan speak live and in person, the strategist in me always wanted to see how his communications played on television. Speeches and debates often appear differently on television than they do in person. Camera angles, jump cuts from candidate to candidate, close-up shots, lighting, and audience reaction shots can all distort the way an event appears.

One of my favorite ways to experience a Reagan speech was to take an informal poll of the reactions and nonverbal responses of the crowd. Sometimes when we were out on the campaign trail I'd work my way through the throng and position myself at an angle where I could look out at the faces of Reagan's audience. If you watched their reactions while listening to him speak, you could pinpoint the exact moment his words touched their hearts and minds. It was like watching electricity flow from its source and through a circuit before electrifying its destination. Reagan's second debate against Walter Mondale was no exception.

When the moment came, Nancy was in the front row looking at him with that famous and sincere loving gaze.

Just as we had anticipated, the question would be asked.

Henry Trewhitt, a reporter for the *Baltimore Sun*, went into his windup. "I recall . . . that President Kennedy had to go for days on end with very little sleep during the Cuban missile crisis. Is there any doubt in your mind that you would be able to function in such circumstances?"

What happened next was pure Reagan.

"Not at all, Mr. Trewhitt. And I want you to know that, also, I will not make age an issue of this campaign. I am not going to exploit, for political purposes, my opponent's youth and inexperience."

Laughter rang out everywhere.

In the auditorium.

Backstage.

In staff hotel rooms.

In my focus group . . .

Even Walter Mondale was laughing. What else was he going to do? If he didn't laugh, he'd look sore. If he did laugh, he would confirm what everyone already knew: Reagan was just getting started; he was up to the task; "You ain't seen nothin' yet!"

None of us knew what he had planned for that moment—it was his line. Always the performer, he liked to surprise even us sometimes.

What wasn't a surprise, however, was that we were going to win big from the start. The closest Mondale ever got to us was just before the Kansas City debate, when he was within eight points. Afterward, Reagan expanded his lead to twenty-one points.

At 4:30 on election morning, I awoke in my room at the Century Plaza to review the last numbers to come in. It was then that I realized just what Ronald Reagan had accomplished.

Not only were we looking at one of the largest landslides in presidential history, we were witnessing the beginning of something much greater and long-lasting: a rolling realignment. Reagan won more than 54 million popular votes and 526 electors. It was a near electoral sweep. Of the fifty states, the only one Mondale captured was his home state of Minnesota. Reagan would have won that state with a switch of just 1,876 votes in a state that had cast over 2 million ballots. Were it not for the Reagans pulling back on the reins out of deference for their opponent, we might have even won that state, too.

Reagan's victory had bumped the chessboard of American politics and sent political preconceptions flying everywhere. Quite simply, he had changed the calculus of American politics. When I crafted the campaign plan for the Reagan-Carter contest in June 1980, 30 percent of registered voters considered themselves to be Republican, 19 percent Independents, and 51 percent Democrats. At the end of the 1984 campaign the difference between Republicans and Democrats was within the statistical margin of error. Indeed, Reagan's ability to reshape the electoral landscape of American presidential politics remains one of his most enduring political legacies.

A month after the election I met with President Reagan in the Oval Office. The president and I seated ourselves side by side before the fire. I told him how very proud I was to have been associated with his election campaign, and he responded by saying how much he appreciated my strategic counsel, the accuracy of my numbers, and my dedication to him. Shortly thereafter we were joined by Baker, Meese, and Deaver.

I began by telling the president that there had been four media myths about the campaign that needed to be dispelled. The first was that the election didn't represent a mandate. I cited the fact that not only had the popular vote been substantial, but that the president's victory had reshaped the playing field considerably. Our 64 percent support among young people and 56 percent support among blue-collar workers were further signs that the "Reagan Democrats" were here to stay.

Second, I tackled the myth that stated we had won only because Reagan was a much beloved individual. "While your Irish smile and twinkling eye were very much appreciated, Mr. President, when I asked people why they voted for you, the dominant responses were that you had done an effective job, that they supported you on the issues, and that you were a strong leader."

The third myth I mentioned was that had turnout only been higher, the race would have been closer. "In point of fact, the number that pleased me most out of the thousands I have looked at over the last four months was generated from interviews among registered voters who did not vote. The number that brought a smile to my face was that 67 percent of the non-voting members of the electorate said they would have cast ballots for you had they gone to the polls. So you would have won by a larger, not smaller, margin."

The last myth generated by the media was that Walter Mondale didn't get his message through. "Mr. President, the problem for Walter Mondale was that he *did* get his message through, and that message set the basis for the landslide."

Never had hope and optimism been higher. Sixty percent of the electorate were saying that America was headed in the right direction, and 70 percent could identify something very specific they felt good would happen with the president in the saddle.

On the other hand, I then said that those expectations were so high that I didn't think they could endure and that one of the challenges we faced was to achieve sufficient success to keep those expectations buoyant.

Baker then spoke up. "Dick, how long do we have before we need to produce some concrete results?"

"Jim, I don't think we have much longer than eight or nine months," I replied. I then recapped by simply saying that I felt a good deal would hinge on what happened in the next few months.

I pointed out to the president that yesterday my wife, Jeralie, and I had been at Harvard. We had spent the rest of the day out at Lexington and Concord and stood at the bridge where the Revolutionary War was initiated. I told him that, as I stood there on that bridge, it occurred to me that Americans, now as then, are willing to sacrifice much if they truly believe those sacrifices will expand hope and opportunity for others.

"Our challenges for the next few months are to show progress, to show action, to further actualize the vision you outlined in the campaign. If that happens, I believe your second term will be a success."

Little did I know just how much sacrifice, as well as success, would be just around the corner.

6

The Best and Worst
of Times

The White House, 1984–1988

---

*My friends, we live in a world that's lit by lightning.
So much is changing and will change, but so much
endures and transcends time.*

—Ronald Reagan, Second Inaugural Address,
January 21, 1985

It was cold.

So cold, in fact, that on January 21, 1985, Ronald Reagan's
second inaugural address had to be delivered inside the
Rotunda of the Capitol. This had not been the president's
preference, of course. Reagan always liked to speak in the
wide-open spaces under an endless sky. But the icy air racing
through Washington, D.C., that morning had confined his
desires and showed no signs of slowing.

Equally unrelenting would be the deluge of advice offered
to President Reagan's new chief of staff, Donald T. Regan.
Regan had landed the job by striking a highly unusual deal

with the former bearer of that title, James Baker. The two men decided they would switch jobs. Some believed Baker had seen the writing on the wall, that he understood the dour history of presidential second terms. These observers concluded that Baker, ever the pragmatist, had decided to leave on a high note. Whatever the case, one thing was certain: we all wanted Ronald Reagan's second term to be a success, and in that spirit, I offered the political neophyte Regan some advice.

Even as the president was still busy delivering his inaugural address in the Capitol, I had sent a memorandum to the newly appointed chief of staff. The document was marked "Personal and Confidential." When I drafted the memo I had no way of knowing that my words would foreshadow future events. Here is an excerpt from that private memorandum:

> You have, Don, a unique opportunity to provide the Reagan second term with the focus and thrust I believe it badly needs. In short, you can significantly enhance the Administration's power, simply defined as 'the ability to make things happen.' Political power defined in these terms over the last two decades has most always been ephemeral. Nevertheless, the unique chemistry between the man (Ronald Reagan) and the moment (1985 through 88) is such that if we can make things happen, we can induce change that will imprint this generation and the next for the better.
>
> Nevertheless, we would be foolish not to recognize that there are tremendous forces that can quickly dissipate that power unless we utilize this next year to maintain and extend the popular mandate that was granted through the 1984 election. . . .
>
> It has been my observation over these last four years that the three essential characteristics needed for men serving the President are, in order, competence, loyalty, and experience. Three years ago I would have probably

not ranked "loyalty" so important. Today, I think it is almost as important as competence.

The second term tries men's loyalty. Don, be careful of selecting persons to serve in the Cabinet or the White House who are "double minded"—persons who have commitments, politically and otherwise, to agendas that go beyond the President's interest.

The man reading my memorandum, Donald T. Regan, had learned everything he knew about leadership and management from the rough-and-tumble world of Wall Street. As a former president of Merrill Lynch, Regan had rocketed to the top of the corporate world. Yet while he had achieved success on the Street, he was, by his own admission, no politician. Don was driven, smart, linear, serious, and, in my view, had the political acuity of a toaster. In many ways he was a tragic figure; his strengths were as great as his weaknesses. Regan, that is to say, was no Reagan.

I remember participating in one of Don's early Oval Office sessions with President Reagan. At one point, Deaver mentioned that the president should be feeling very good now that he had someone his own age (Regan) to play with. The president and Don had other things in common, too. For example, they were both of Irish descent. But age and ethnicity aside, they were complete opposites. I never felt Don Regan had sinister motives or desired to diminish the president's standing. It was just that his values, interests, temperament, vision, and ability to communicate with others seemed diametrically opposed to President Reagan's.

And there was another problem. I detected a noticeable difference in the president when Regan was in the room. President Reagan's mood would become serious and restrained. He was much less open and free than I had ever seen him. It was startling.

To be sure, Don tried to be more like Reagan. If he just learned to mimic the president's love for laughter, he thought, perhaps he could win him over. So the new chief of staff would force himself to tell jokes during our meetings with the president, and sometimes Reagan would even laugh at his punch lines. But soon the former corporate raider reverted back to his old habits of seriousness and a no-nonsense attitude that stood in sharp contrast to the president's warm and affable nature. I think Don misread Ronald Reagan the same way others had done throughout the president's life. Erroneously, he believed that the source of Reagan's communicative abilities were external, capable of being emulated, and superficial. But they weren't. They came from within. They came from his values. And the trouble was, Reagan's values weren't Regan's values.

Still, President Reagan felt he could get along with anyone, and he respected those who had survived and thrived in the competitive world of the financial markets. So Don was given a chance. Besides, at the beginning of the second term it seemed little could derail the Reagan Revolution. The day following his inauguration, the president enjoyed a commanding 72 percent job approval rating. The economy was humming and America was at peace. What could possibly go wrong?

Well, I could think of two things. Just after his landslide victory I told the president that there were two worries that kept me awake at night. Reagan responded, "Dick, defense is one. What's the other one?"

"Economic growth," I said.

The forward lean of the Reagan Revolution, I believed, was contingent on maintaining the peace and prosperity he had achieved during his first term.

As it turned out, President Reagan's second term would contain one glaring failure bookended by several historic successes. From 1985 to 1989, the Greatest Communicator would deliver speeches the world would always remember, as well as some—about Iran-contra—he wished the could forget. But beyond the artistry of Ronald Reagan's words, he would accomplish things—incredible things.

Indeed, President Reagan's second term would come to represent the best and worst of times.

During the first year of Reagan's second term, the president received an opportunity to begin making good on his dream of fostering a more peaceful world. The United States and the Soviet Union had convened a summit in Geneva to discuss how the two countries might begin reducing the number of strategic nuclear missiles that each had pointed at the other. While Reagan cautioned that the creation of "Star Wars" might take a lifetime, he believed there was much that could be done in the interim to reduce the danger created by the nuclear sword hanging over the world, with these Strategic Arms Reduction Talks (START) being an important first step toward changing the cold war equation. Successful negotiations, however, would require an honest broker, and Ronald Reagan thought he might have one in a fifty-four-year-old Soviet leader by the name of Mikhail Gorbachev.

But why would Reagan, a president who had significantly ratcheted up the defense budget, destroy that which he had worked so hard to create? And why would the Soviet Union, a country that had willfully engaged in an arms race with the United States, agree to do the same?

For the Russians, the answer was simple: Star Wars had forced General Secretary Gorbachev's hand just as Reagan had hoped it might. Gorbachev understood that the creation of a program like Star Wars would break the Russian piggy bank as it became impossible for the Soviet Union to keep pace with American expenditures in a "high rollers" arms race. Gorbachev had to know full well that a Marxist economy like his was no match for the miracle of free-market capitalism that fueled the U.S. economy.

For Reagan, START combined with the development of Star Wars would represent the chance to work toward peace. For Gorbachev, fewer arms meant expending fewer resources on defense, and that, in turn, would help ease the pressure on an already rickety Soviet economy.

And that's why Ronald Reagan and Mikhail Gorbachev's meeting in Geneva became such an axial event. It wasn't long before that President Reagan had declared Gorbachev's Soviet Union an "evil empire." How each man would interact when meeting face-to-face would impact future negotiations between the two superpowers.

But there was another reason Geneva was important for Reagan. The summit gave him the chance to challenge the negative image constructed by his opponents, an image we'd been battling his entire career. Instead of being portrayed as a gunslinging cowboy whose finger hovered carelessly above the "red button," he would have the chance to project himself as the world leader he truly was—an American president in command of a responsible, action-oriented, and diplomatically savvy foreign policy.

Achieving this goal, however, would require that he employ the full resources of his communicative arsenal. You mustn't forget that Reagan had honed his negotiating skills during his days as president of the Screen Actors Guild (SAG). If Reagan could negotiate with movie studios, producers, and actors—a group with some of the biggest egos on the planet—he could negotiate with almost anyone. And it would be this component of President Reagan's rhetorical leadership—his ability to communicate not just onstage, but interpersonally, one on one, with the leader of the Soviet Union—that reflects the difference between being merely a great communicator and being one of the greatest.

A little over a month before the president traveled to Geneva, we met in the Oval Office. There, I told him I believed public attitudes were ripe for a successful summit. American expectations were reasonable and not too high. Also, the actions of the Soviets were viewed by most Americans as propaganda. The public was hungry to witness more person-to-person contact, and they wanted to see an increase in the number and variety of communications between our two countries. In other words, they were eager to see President Reagan reach out and bridge the divide while at the same time displaying strong, decisive, and principled leadership.

Our plan was for the president to rhetorically frame the Geneva summit by delivering two major presidential speeches, one before the summit and another after it. The first of these was delivered on October 24, 1985, to the fortieth session of the United Nations General Assembly in New York. The second would be a live prime-time address scheduled for November 21, 1985, to a joint session of Congress.

President Reagan's UN speech had gone well. Now, on November 14, 1985, just two days before his departure for Geneva, the president, his chief of staff, and I would have a final meeting to review the communications strategy one last time before his face-to-face encounter with Mikhail Gorbachev.

I arrived at the White House just a little before my 4:30 p.m. meeting with President Reagan. As I made my way to the Oval Office, I stopped to visit briefly with the president's secretary, Kathy Osborne. While we were chatting, someone delivered fourteen pens, the kind you typically see the president use one at a time when signing a bill or important document. The reason presidents use so many pens is so they can give them to friends and associates as souvenirs.

"I was a little optimistic in ordering fourteen, I suppose," said Kathy.

"What do you mean?" I asked.

While opening and testing each one to ensure it worked, she responded, "Well, Dick, I'm going to take these to Geneva with us in the hopes that there will be enough documents to generate plenty of souvenir pens."

Don Regan arrived a few minutes later. We walked into the president's office together. Reagan was seated behind the projection screen that the White House staff would set up before most of my presentations. The president playfully peeked around the screen, smiled, and said, "Hello there, Mr. Wirthlin." It was the first time in my recollection that he had ever referred to me by my last name.

He had on a dark suit, a red "power" tie, and a very white shirt—more on that in a second. We made our way toward the couches and chairs. As we sat down, in reference to Geneva, I said, "Well, Mr. President, do you have on your traveling shoes?"

He twisted his shoe toward himself, looked at it, and then realized I was talking about Geneva. Chuckling, he said, "Oh, yes, Dick, I've been getting my bags all packed. I've decided I'm only going to take blue suits to the summit. That way I won't have to worry about getting the right socks and only have to take a few ties. You know, I wear my shirts for two days. So I'll only need three or four shirts plus one extra in the event we have an unforeseen problem of some kind or another."

Don Regan, a man who had never lost the sartorial flair of Wall Street, looked mortified. "Well, Mr. President, how can you possibly do that?" he quipped somewhat sharply. "I mean, I wear two shirts every *day*, one for the business hours and then one to look fresh at night."

Talk about a culture clash. It was Dixon, Illinois, versus New York City.

The president looked a little shocked. He leaned forward and said, "Well, Don, doesn't this shirt look all right? This is my second day for this same shirt."

Here we were, two days before the president's showdown with the leader of the second most powerful military in the universe, and we were locked in a heated debate over the finer points of travel packing protocol.

This was too good to pass up; I had to jump in. "Actually,

I'm with you, Mr. President. I have to confess, I sometimes wear my shirts twice, too."

Reagan shot his chief of staff a look that said, "Take that, Don!"

And then, at the risk of giving away highly sensitive national security information, the president made a startling revelation. "And, of course, I only take two pairs of boxer shorts."

Don's eyes bulged.

"They're made out of that nylon and I just kind of rinse them out at night, dry them up, and that way I can travel lightly," said the president.

I thought Don Regan was going to have a heart attack.

Reagan continued, "Another thing I find helpful is to put all of the shirts on one hanger; that way you don't have to take too many hangers."

Don looked aghast. "Well . . . but . . . don't they get all wrinkled when you fold them over?"

"Not that I've noticed," said the president. "They seem to do just fine."

I jumped back in: "Maybe when the president finishes his term we should all collaborate and write a book on handy travel tips."

Everyone laughed.

"Of course, when the royal couple came here they brought ten tons of baggage!" said Reagan.

"I know," I said. "They travel as if they are still being taken from point to point by the Royal Navy."

"True," said the president. "But, on the other hand, Nancy has been packing for over three months now!"

With the real danger confronting the civilized world— excessive packing—now behind us, I presented my findings. Of all the numbers I shared with him that day, the one that interested him most was that his job rating dealing with the Soviets had gone from 50 in September to 67. I closed the session by telling President Reagan that my own personal hopes and prayers would go with him to Geneva as well as those of millions of Americans. He thanked me and said he was on his way to get a shot for his "sniffles."

"I'll see you after the summit, Mr. President. Good luck."

He then walked out the door leading to the Rose Garden on his way to get his shot.

Once in Geneva, Reagan gained initial visual advantage when the president, a man twenty years General Secretary Gorbachev's senior, greeted him in the bone-chilling cold without an overcoat. Gorbachev, on the other hand, was wrapped in a heavy coat, scarf, and hat. The contrast sent a signal of Reagan's strength and vigor.

The negotiations began, and before long it became clear the two men were interested in building a relationship. For two countries that had been deadlocked in the grip of the cold war, this was a significant development. And that's when, in a moment of interpersonal goodwill, President Reagan decided to see whether achieving his primary objective— forging a personal bond between himself and Gorbachev—was possible.

Our team had scouted out a little summerhouse overlooking a lake where the two leaders could meet. Reagan extended the invitation and Gorbachev accepted. With only their security personnel, interpreters, and a photographer in tow, the two men walked to the summerhouse. There they sat in cushy chairs in front of a crackling fire and did what Reagan had come to do: build a relationship.

If you stop and think about it, so much of a president's success is contingent on his ability to communicate interpersonally. It's one of those dimensions of rhetorical leadership that is difficult for us as voters to get a handle on before electing a president. This is unfortunate, because while a presidential contender might be a great speaker, effective from the podium, determining whether he is a great communicator can only be done by analyzing his ability to connect with individuals in a one-on-one setting.

During the summit's official meetings some minor items would be negotiated. But the real victory occurred when both Reagan and Gorbachev agreed to visit each other's countries to continue talking about START. It was settled—the dialogue would continue.

When President Reagan returned home, the American people embraced him with warmth and affection. As he stood to speak before a joint session of Congress, he received a hero's welcome.

> I called for a fresh start, and we made that start. I can't claim that we had a meeting of the minds on such fundamentals as ideology or national purpose, but we understand each other better, and that's a key to peace. . . . Specifically, we agreed in Geneva that each side should move to cut offensive nuclear arms by 50 percent in appropriate categories. In our joint statement we called for early progress on this, turning the talks toward our chief goal—offensive reductions. We called for an interim accord on intermediate-range nuclear forces, leading, I hope, to the complete elimination of this class of missiles— and all of this with tough verification.
>
> We are also opening a dialog on combating the spread and use of chemical weapons, while moving to ban them altogether. . . . Mr. Gorbachev insisted that we might use a strategic defense system to put offensive weapons into space and establish nuclear superiority. I made it clear that SDI has nothing to do with offensive weapons; that, instead, we are investigating non-nuclear defense systems that would only threaten offensive missiles, not people. If our research succeeds, it will bring much closer the safer, more stable world that we seek. Nations could defend themselves against missile attack and mankind, at long

last, escape the prison of mutual terror. And this is my dream. . . .

We know that peace is not just the absence of war. We don't want a phony peace or a frail peace. We didn't go in pursuit of some kind of illusory detente. We can't be satisfied with cosmetic improvements that won't stand the test of time. We want real peace.

After the speech I drafted a memorandum for the president. "Seldom have you given a speech, Mr. President, when both your immediate audience and the national television audience have been so positively disposed toward you, personally, and what you have accomplished," I wrote. I also informed him that the day after his address, my national study showed that 77 percent of all Americans approved of the way he was handling his job as president, 76 percent approved of the way he was handling relations with the Soviet Union, and an amazing 81 percent approved of the way he handled the Geneva summit.

But while Geneva may have begun easing tensions between the United States and the Soviet Union, it had the opposite effect on my relationship with some of the president's speechwriters. The reason: PulseLine.

During the second term I began frequent use of another instrument designed to assist the president in maximizing the power of his rhetoric. I called it PulseLine. Here's how it worked.

Whenever the president was to deliver a major policy speech, I would gather a group of between thirty-five and one hundred Americans. Selection of these individuals was based on the target audience we were interested in studying. For example, if we wanted to gauge how males under 50 years old reacted to the president and his rhetoric, we could arrange for a group of men fitting this description to participate in our study. Participants would be handed a small handheld electronic box with a rheostat (dial) on its face that ran from zero to ten. Each of these devices was connected to a central tabulation unit. Participants were then told they would watch a speech. When the speaker said something they responded positively to, they were to turn their dial toward ten to indicate their level of agreement. Conversely, negative reactions were to be registered by turning the dial toward zero.

After the speech was finished, the central tabulation unit would average the participants' overall ratings as well as provide a measure of the degree of consensus in the rating of the group. The printout looked like a mountain range, complete with peaks and valleys. I could then go back and pinpoint the exact phrases and segments from the president's speech that had produced the most and least favorable responses, matching the speech's highs and lows against the actual videotape of the event. This allowed me to track how the audience had responded almost to the president's every word. Mind you, this was all done with the full understanding that PulseLine, like any research instrument, was limited in what it could and couldn't measure. Nevertheless, the tool could help provide us with a context for understanding the magic of the Reagan message.

Also—and this is important—we would then hold focus groups with these same individuals to tap into the *reasons* for their responses. We wanted to understand the emotional dimensions behind why a viewer had dialed toward ten or toward zero. The result was a list of something I called "power phrases," which were those lines or phrases from the speech that had garnered the highest response from the audience. I saw to it that subsequent speeches on similar issues contained these power phrases, and statements by White House surrogates or daily talking points could also benefit from their use.

And that's what I had done when President Reagan spoke to a joint session of Congress following his return from Geneva.

The original PulseLine was conducted on his speech to the United Nations General Assembly in New York, roughly a month before the Geneva summit. Three power phrases emerged from that speech: "fresh start," "escape the prison of mutual terror," and "peace and progress." You will notice the inclusion of the first and second power phrases in the excerpt above from the prime-time speech after the summit. That, in a nutshell, was PulseLine: it allowed us to keep what worked and change what didn't.

Some of the president's speechwriters appreciated PulseLine. They saw the benefit it provided both to them and the president. But others, I was sad to learn, didn't feel the same way. I suppose they viewed PulseLine as an attempt to turn art into science, to treat the ancient craft of rhetoric like a marketing project. But that was never my intent.

In fact, PulseLine took its cues from speechwriters, not the other way around. The instrument merely did what all speechwriters do when they sit in the back of a room taking down tally marks of a speaker's strongest applause lines. As any wordsmith will tell you, for a speech to resonate, you have to analyze your audience. Moreover, when a line doesn't work or falls flat, you must refine it until it touches hearts and minds. That's what PulseLine was designed to do: record those areas of greatest impact and point out which lines muddled the president's message.

Not surprisingly, President Reagan was intrigued by PulseLine. He saw the value of being able to pinpoint areas of strength and weakness in his speeches. He'd been doing it all his life. After all, repetition of the same winning message had been his bread and butter. The address he delivered in 1964 for Barry Goldwater is often called "The Speech." The reason: Reagan basically only *had* one speech! Once he found something that worked, he stuck with it. PulseLine gave him a faster way of knowing whether his phrases were having their desired impact. What's more, he was confident enough in his own abilities not to take it personally when the trend lines dipped. The way he saw it, it was better to know what areas needed improvement. He wanted to make sure that his audiences received his messages clearly.

Still, I can see how some speechwriters might have felt PulseLine was a way of "judging" their writing abilities. I never wanted any of them to feel that way—not ever. Without disparaging the fine efforts of other speechwriting shops from other presidential administrations, I believe to this day that President Reagan's speechwriters were, hands down, the best team of speechwriters for any president in American history. Not only had they arrived at the White House with impressive individual skills but, most importantly, they loved the man for whom they wrote. They believed deeply in the principles for which he fought. They didn't just write his speeches on "autopilot." They infused their writing with the same passion they felt for him in their hearts. They wrote *up* to him, not *down*. It made all the difference in the world and helped him generate strong momentum.

In fact, entering 1986, we had incredible support. The president had led well. And Americans knew it. During our January 21 meeting, Reagan seemed unusually cheerful.

Just days earlier, he had undertaken a physical examination at Bethesda. Thankfully, the doctor's reports showed only tiny benign polyps in his colon. Reagan said the thing that fascinated him most was the CAT scan. With a twinkle in his eye, he told me that the young, attractive nurse who reviewed the CAT scan had said, "Mr. President, you have the insides of a man twenty years younger." He liked that.

I then told him that it wasn't just his insides that were looking good. According to the American people, they liked what they were seeing on the outside as well. That day I left the Oval Office having presented the best set of numbers I had ever taken to Ronald Reagan over our then eighteen-year history. These were, indeed, some of the best times for the president and the country.

But they would be short-lived.

Exactly one week following our meeting, America experienced one of its worst times. In the midst of tragedy, the Greatest Communicator would be tested.

We had worked tirelessly on the president's 1986 State of the Union address. States of the Union are always a massive undertaking. Everyone wants a hand in the process, and, as a consequence, it's not uncommon for a president's speech to go through a dozen or more drafts until most everyone is satisfied with the final product.

When January 28, the date of Reagan's State of the Union address, finally rolled around, we were all anxious to see the president breathe life into the speech that so many had helped create. But it was not to be, at least not then.

Because that was the fateful day when the space shuttle *Challenger* would incinerate in midflight, taking with it the lives of seven astronauts. Even as you read these lines, I imagine your mind is replaying that awful scene of a Y-shaped trail of smoke scarring a clear blue Florida sky. The image remains etched in our collective consciousness, and I can tell you it pained Ronald Reagan to his core.

Equally painful was that many of the nation's children were watching the launch that day. Christa McAuliffe, a schoolteacher, was one of the *Challenger* seven, and thus NASA had encouraged science teachers to let their students watch the event. In an instant, millions of American children were confronted with a concept they had never faced: mortality.

The president's decision to postpone his State of the Union address was made quickly. I was in Chicago when I received a call from the White House. I was told the president was considering postponing his State of the Union address and wanted my opinion. I agreed entirely with his impulse and felt the constitutionally required message should be rescheduled.

That night, instead of a policy speech, millions of Americans watched as their president delivered live from the Oval Office a simple message filled with grace, sorrow, and hope. Reagan also did something unique that evening, something American presidents seldom do during a nationally televised speech: he spoke directly to America's children.

Seeming to look through our television screens, the president said:

> And I want to say something to the schoolchildren of America who were watching the live coverage of the shuttle's takeoff. I know it is hard to understand, but sometimes painful things like this happen. It's all part of the process of exploration and discovery. It's all part of taking a chance and expanding man's horizons. The future doesn't belong to the fainthearted; it belongs to the brave. The *Challenger* crew was pulling us into the future, and we'll continue to follow them.

The *Challenger* tragedy had left American children with big questions and broken hearts. As a father, Reagan could remember how difficult it had been to explain to his daughter Patty why her goldfish weren't swimming. Now millions of American parents would be faced with a task much greater, and he wanted to do what little he could to help them.

At the close of his speech, the president ended with words most of us will never forget. He said, "The crew of the space shuttle *Challenger* honored us by the manner in which they lived their lives. We will never forget them, nor the last time we saw them, this morning, as they prepared for the journey and waved goodbye and 'slipped the surly bonds of earth' to 'touch the face of God.'"

The *Challenger* speech is just one instance of Ronald Reagan's rare gift for communicating caring in times of deep sorrow and emotion. Peggy Noonan, the speechwriter who penned the speech, had captured Reagan's voice and values beautifully. Indeed, the president's ability to speak on behalf of the nation in such convincing and sympathetic tones was in itself an act of service. But over the years I would sometimes wonder how he did it. How could he intone such emotion without becoming emotional?

I received my answer two years earlier in the wake of the president's stirring speech marking the fortieth anniversary of D-Day. Standing before the U.S. Ranger Monument at Pointe du Hoc, France, the president had served us again. This time he had come to look into the faces of former soldiers who, forty years earlier, had scaled the cliffs of Normandy as boys and left them as men. He said:

> Behind me is a memorial that symbolizes the Ranger daggers that were thrust into the top of these cliffs. And before me are the men who put them there.
>
> These are the boys of Pointe du Hoc. These are the men who took the cliffs. These are the champions who helped free a continent. These are the heroes who helped end a war.
>
> Gentlemen, I look at you and I think of the words of Stephen Spender's poem. You are men who in your "lives fought for life . . . and left the vivid air signed with your honor."

During moments like these—the fortieth anniversary of D-Day and the *Challenger* explosion—Reagan graced us with another aspect of his communicative greatness, one that is easily overlooked. And here it is: he spoke *for* us when we were too choked up to speak for ourselves.

Don't miss the significance of that statement.

When someone is delivering a speech at a time of sorrow, one of two things typically happens. One, the speaker becomes so overwrought with emotion that he or she breaks down. Or two, the speaker emotionally detaches himself to such a degree that he appears cold and distant.

Yet Reagan did neither.

Instead he reflected the emotions swirling inside us and at the same time maintained his composure. And in this, he became a pillar of strength for us to lean on. "How is he feeling inside right now?" I asked myself. "How does he do it?"

After his trip to Normandy, I became so curious about these questions that I finally asked him directly. I wanted to know how he could deliver his words flawlessly without getting swept away by his own emotions. I needed to understand how he could look into the faces of those men who had traveled thousands of miles to revisit a place that, after all those years, their hearts and minds and fears had never really left.

So I asked him.

Reagan confessed it wasn't easy. But he explained that he had developed a method that worked for him. In preparing for a highly emotional speech, the president said he would devote extra hours to practice, rehearsing the speech several times. The first run-throughs were often difficult to complete without getting choked up. But, take after take, line after line, he said, he would begin to slowly suppress his inner emotions, while still taking pains to ensure that his voice and outward appearance reflected his true feelings. Then he would home in on those passages that were highly emotional. He would rehearse them again and again, until he could deliver them without a crack in his voice or a tear in his eye.

Hearing him explain his method reminded me of a boxer landing blows against his own body. On our behalf, he had trained himself to take the pain.

If you've ever seen a friend or loved one break down while delivering a eulogy, you know that awful feeling. You want to rush to their side, wrap your arms around them, and rescue them by saying the words they can't say for themselves.

Momentarily, you may even contemplate doing so. But in the end, you stay seated. Like the struggling eulogist, you come to realize that the lump in your throat and the tears flooding your eyes have paralyzed you as well.

In America's times of need, Reagan swallowed the lump in his throat, dried his eyes, and went before the nation to say the things we needed him to. He possessed this ability not because he was an actor, but because he had already dealt with the pain behind closed doors. He did it so that he might become our voice.

Maybe it was this dimension of Reagan—his tenderness and wide-eyed optimism—that gave the Soviet Union and its leaders the wrong impression. Perhaps they believed that if given the chance he would compromise Star Wars in exchange for a reduction in the Soviet nuclear arsenal. But if Mikhail Gorbachev had any doubts about the president's resolve to not just end but *win* the cold war, they were squelched during the two leaders' much-anticipated meeting in Reykjavik, Iceland.

For this was to be the place where President Reagan and Mikhail Gorbachev would make good on the commitments they had made in Geneva to reduce both countries' strategic nuclear weapons arsenals. Like that earlier meeting, Reykjavik stood to influence perceptions about Reagan's commitment toward achieving peace. But perhaps most importantly, it would provide America with an unvarnished look at Soviet intentions.

Ten days before his departure, I told the president and his chief of staff that Reagan's public pronouncements before and after Reykjavik would crystallize public perceptions. I counseled the administration to consistently refer to Reykjavik as a "pre-summit" meeting. I did this for two reasons. First, it was more accurate; Reykjavik was not a summit in the traditional sense of the word. Second, framing the meeting as a "pre-summit" gave us leverage in defining expectations for future summits.

I told the president that the meeting should be positioned as a litmus test of the Soviet Union's commitment to START. The first step had been getting the Soviets to discuss arms reduction. This goal having been accomplished, I said our message should be that the pre-summit would reveal Gorbachev's level of seriousness about arms reduction. If the meeting furthered negotiations, the general secretary was serious. If not, he wasn't. In other words, by establishing compliance as the standard for success, we could apply pressure to promote peace.

Finally, regardless of how the negotiations turned out, I strongly advised the president to address the nation immediately following his return from Iceland. Given the success of his post-Geneva speech, this took little convincing.

On October 11, 1986, Gorbachev and Reagan began meeting in a small, unassuming building known as Hofdi House. Early on the discussions seemed to hold promise for something truly historic. Gorbachev, it appeared, was prepared to match the United States' willingness to drastically reduce stocks of just about every class of nuclear weapons, including intermediate-range missiles. Deliberations had been going well—great, in fact. The two leaders were on the verge of rewriting history.

That is, until Gorbachev decided to pull the rug out from beneath the president. The general secretary said that their historic agreement would, of course, be contingent on U.S. agreement not to move forward with testing Star Wars outside the laboratory.

Reagan was incensed.

Here, at the eleventh hour, the Soviets' intentions had been laid bare. They had brought Reagan to Reykjavik to kill Star Wars. It mattered little that the president had offered to share emerging technology with them. From the Russian vantage point, what good were blueprints if you couldn't afford the materials necessary to use them? Gorbachev understood that

Star Wars—the "peace shield," as President Reagan sometimes called it——could mean the end of the Soviet Union's ability to keep pace with the United States militarily.

And so did Reagan.

When the two men emerged from Hofdi House, they were greeted with a flurry of flashbulbs and a gaggle of anxious reporters. President Reagan's countenance told the story— there would be no deal. He wasn't about to cave in to Soviet demands. He stood firm. The United States and the Soviet Union would leave Iceland with no agreement and no assur-ances of future summits.

As Nancy recalls in her autobiography, *My Turn*, when the president returned home he told her that at the end of their session Gorbachev said, "I don't know what more I could have done."

"I do," said Reagan. "You could have said yes."

As soon as the talks ended, the media began casting Reykjavik as a massive failure of American foreign policy. *Alas,* they thought, *Reagan's diffident, unbending, cowboy style has finally cost the world its greatest chance for peace.* But in point of fact, Reagan's principled decision in Iceland had revealed to Gorbachev a fundamental lesson: Ronald Reagan meant what he said. In time, the president's willingness to hold fast in the face of blistering criticism would ultimately pave the path for peace.

But that would come later. In the immediate aftermath, I was adamant that we get out in front of the story. We needed to rewrite the media script and explain to the American people that the president's meeting with Gorbachev wasn't a failure— it was a success. That the president would not submit to Soviet demands had been the ultimate act of leadership. Of course, the elite media and most Democrats scoffed at this notion. They thought Reagan had finally been pinned to the ground. But, as always, the American people would have the final say.

Upon his return, the president delivered an address from the Oval Office as planned. I had been tracking American views before, during, and after the event. Prior to his meeting with Gorbachev, Reagan's approval rating stood at 64 percent. Following his speech, that number rose to 70 percent.

Americans understood what the elite media and the Democrats never could: Ronald Reagan would never sacrifice peace on the altar of popularity. Ironically, in taking this stand, the president gained the very thing he had risked most—public approval. As long as I had known him, his view had always been that if he took a hit in the polls because of his support for a cause he believed was in the best interests of the country, so be it. His willingness to eschew that which seemed the most politically advantageous was one of the things Americans loved about him. His presidency wasn't one big photo op, as his critics would have had the world believe. While the doubters called him naïve, Reagan believed leadership was about changing the world.

The president's foreign policy agenda had resonated with voters. So less than two weeks later, Reagan sought to transfer that support elsewhere when he pivoted from international relations to economic issues, namely tax policy. With the passage of the 1986 Tax Reform Act, he captured the crown jewel of his domestic agenda in the second term.

The bill reduced marginal rates from the 70 percent they had been under his predecessor to two tiers: 28 percent and 15 percent. Also, by this time inflation, the nemesis of economic growth, had been reduced to 1 percent. The confluence of these economic realities meant that even as tax rates were plummeting, total revenues collected by the Internal Revenue Service had increased by some 50 percent after adjusting for inflation. Investors had more money to invest. And they did. Critics of so-called Reaganomics were left scratching their heads.

But again, the president always celebrated his administration's economic achievements not because Americans had more money but because they had more of the things money represents. All along, Reagan's vision was to restore a sense of fairness and personal incentive to U.S. tax policies. He believed that a system that punished entrepreneurialism, hard work, and risk-taking was destined to failure. So he inverted that logic. In so doing, he unshackled the lion of free-market capitalism.

Another often overlooked feature of his 1986 reforms is what the bill did for taxpayers at the lower levels of the economic ladder. Although his detractors would never admit it, Ronald Reagan's economic reforms represented one of the most compassionate "social programs" imaginable.

For one, passage of Reagan's Fair Share Tax Bill meant that six million citizens in the lowest income brackets who had paid taxes in the past would not pay *any* taxes in the future. By allowing these individuals to keep all of what they earned, Reagan rewarded those Americans who played by the rules, worked hard, and were striving toward greater economic independence.

Second, after Reagan's tax reforms had taken root for two years, the president's policies produced the lowest unemployment rate in fourteen years. In Reagan's book, the best social program ever invented was a job. Not only did it equip individuals with the means to take care of themselves and those they loved, but work produced a sense of pride, discipline, and self-esteem. As a boy, the president had seen how the Great Depression ravaged not only wallets but individuals' sense of self-worth as well. By removing the barriers to job growth, he believed he could reignite America's economic engine. He was right.

The halcyon days of President Reagan's achievements in foreign and domestic policy would not go undeterred, however. Just as quickly as his job approval had soared, it would soon nosedive to the lowest level in years.

As most Reaganauts agree, the Iran-contra affair represented the single most glaring failure of leadership and communication during the administration's eight-year run. While the issue has been well covered, I believe there were several key communicative lessons learned during that period.

At the time and even today, many Americans remain unclear as to what the so-called Iran-contra affair was all about. Part of the confusion stems from the fact that there were actually two separate covert operations involved.

The "Iran" half of the term denotes American negotiations with Iran as a conduit for gaining the release of American hostages being held in Lebanon. The "contra" side of the equation refers to the president's stated policies toward the battle in Nicaragua between the pro-democracy contras and the pro-Marxist Sandinistas. The Reagan administration's support—both politically and militarily—for the contra freedom fighters, therefore, explains the term's inclusion in the phrase "Iran-contra."

The president's high-profile strategy to sway public opinion on aid to the contras in March 1986 failed to generate popular support for his $100 million package. In the wake of this defeat, the president and I met in the Oval Office. There, I informed Reagan that we had experienced the sharpest fall ever for his handling of foreign policy. "I bet I know where it comes from—Nicaragua," he said. "Americans just don't want to spend money abroad."

He was right. Of all the issues Americans said they wanted to allocate funds toward, foreign aid was at the bottom. Still, the lack of support for Reagan's backing of the contras also reflected the so-called Vietnam syndrome. With memories of Vietnam still fresh in their minds, voters were wary of intervening in the internal affairs of a sovereign country, especially one they knew little about.

I pointed out to the president and Don Regan that while the Sandinistas definitely wore "black hats" as far as Americans were concerned, the contras clearly didn't wear "white hats." The majority of citizens saw neither group in a terribly favorable light.

But the whole issue had made Reagan's views on Nicaragua and his desire not to give the Soviet Union a toehold in Central America known to the world and to those in his administration.

Allegations of a potential scandal arose when it appeared that the United States had sold arms to Iran in exchange for putting pressure on the extremists holding American hostages in Lebanon, and that the profits from these transactions were then diverted to fund the contras in Nicaragua. If true, these actions may have broken laws prohibiting the sale of arms to hostage takers. But the central questions were: Did President Reagan knowingly approve a plan he knew to be illegal? And was there a cover-up?

The story broke at the end of November 1986. Like most Americans, I was surprised by the allegations. Around that time I had been admitted to the hospital for surgery. As I was recovering in a hospital bed, I received a call from the Reagans. Both Nancy and the president were on the line, and each wished me a speedy recovery. I told them how much my family had appreciated the flowers they had sent.

The discussion then shifted to Iran-contra. They asked whether I had been able to keep up with the unfolding events. I told them that I had my people tracking the issue closely, but that I had only been able to pick up bits and pieces from newspapers and television while confined to my bed. Truth be told, at this time I was still reeling from the pain medication and probably not in the best shape to be offering counsel to the president of the United States. But when Reagan asked for my bottom-line assessment, I gave it to him.

"Mr. President," I said, "I think the sharks are circling and they smell blood in the water."

We finished up our call and I went back to recuperating.

Well, a day or two later I was reading the *Washington Post* when I noticed an article by Reagan biographer Lou Cannon and reporter David Hoffman. Writing about the president's response to the crisis, they attributed a quote to Reagan that about took my breath away: "'I've never seen the sharks circling like they are now with blood in the water,' the president said in remarkably blunt language."

Even in my groggy state, I should have known better. Reagan often soaked up colorful language like a sponge. And sometimes, especially when he was revved up about something, those colorful locutions would tumble from his lips. Indeed, if the Greatest Communicator had one weakness it was that he sometimes let his emotions drive his message. The allegations of wrongdoing had made him angry. He perceived them as political posturing and opportunism.

But most importantly, I can say without the slightest hesitation, in his heart of hearts Ronald Reagan believed he had done nothing wrong. As the Tower and Walsh commissions did their work, however, he came to realize that operatives working in the shadows had crossed ethical and possibly legal boundaries. Don Regan (who would be replaced as chief of staff), although he had no direct involvement in the issue, was cited by some for not having been attentive enough to know what people were telling his president. Others believed that a small group of mid-level operatives, freelancing on their own, had interpreted the president's stated support for the contras as a "green light" to find a way to fund the freedom fighters in their battle against Communist domination.

But however you looked at it, from start to finish, Iran-contra represented a failure of communication, one that threatened to erode President Reagan's longest and strongest political asset: the bond of trust and credibility he had forged with the American people throughout his political career.

On March 2, 1987, the president, his son, Ron Reagan, the newly installed chief of staff, Howard Baker, and I met in the Oval Office. I believe Baker was exactly the right man for the job. As you may recall, he was the valiant Republican senator who during the Watergate trials posed that now famous question: "What did the president know and when did he know it?" He had a well-earned reputation for integrity and fair dealing. Moreover, he cared about Ronald Reagan and believed in the president's vision for America.

When it was time for me to present my findings, I began, as I often did, by telling the president that I had some bad news and some good news. The bad news was that his job approval rating was as low as it had been during the third year of his first term. I reminded him of the circumstances of the recession and the economic challenges we had faced then that had driven his numbers so low. On Iran, I told him bluntly that Americans simply didn't believe he had been unaware of the diversion of funds. Moreover, they strongly objected to the exchange of arms for hostages and they believed that is exactly what occurred.

The good news, on the other hand, was that even though voters were concerned about foreign policy, they still liked him personally. They were eager to move on to other things, and the issue appeared to be fading as a top priority. But enough Americans viewed Iran-contra as a problem that compromised the president's honesty and integrity.

I then made my strategic recommendation. I joined those voices that had advised the president that he should consider admitting clearly and openly to the American people that the policy was a mistake. Furthermore, I said that he should do so along much the same lines as President John F. Kennedy had done following the Bay of Pigs. I then pointed out the large proportion of people who felt that President Reagan wasn't telling the truth. As the words fell from my lips, he just sat there shaking his head in dismay. For a man who had built his career on the pillars of honesty and trust, it was one of the single most painful things I could say to him. It stung me to do so, especially in front of his son.

And yet Reagan remained calm and didn't rail against what I said. It reminded me of a story he had once told me about the time one of his favorite horses got enmeshed in a tangle of barbed wire. He said that as he struggled to free the animal, it thrashed so violently that with each jerk of its muscles it dug the barbs deeper into its flesh. "What I learned from the experience, Dick, is that sometimes the best way to handle a difficult situation is not to thrash against circumstance. Sometimes it's just better to listen to those that would help you back to safety," he said.

Still, I couldn't leave things on such a dour note. I told him that 78 percent of voters liked him personally, thus providing us with a base for recovery. And then, as I had seen my mentor do all those years, I tried to "leave them laughing" by closing the meeting with a reading of an old Irish blessing. It went like this:

> May those who love us, love us
> And those that don't love us
> May God turn their hearts
> And if he doesn't turn their hearts
> May he turn their ankle
> So we'll know them by their limping

Howard, Ron, the president, and I laughed heartily.

We stood up and began saying our goodbyes. And then, while caught in the throes of one of the most difficult periods of his presidency, the Greatest Communicator concluded that he couldn't disappoint his audience.

"You know, you said there was some good news and some bad news. . . . Have you heard the story about the Ayatollah Khomeni's sister?" he asked.

"No, Mr. President, I don't believe I have," I replied.

"The good news is that she has passed away. The bad news is that she was 156 years old when she did so."

On that note, the meeting ended.

Two days later, President Reagan delivered his apologia to the nation.

For the past three months, I've been silent on the revelations about Iran. And you must have been thinking: "Well, why doesn't he tell us what's happening?" Why doesn't he just speak to us as he has in the past when we've faced troubles and tragedies?" Well, the reason I haven't spoken to you before now is this: You deserve the truth. And as frustrating as the waiting has been, I felt it was improper to come to you with sketchy reports, or possibly even erroneous statements. . . . I've paid a price for my silence in terms of your trust and confidence. But I've had to wait, as you have, for the complete story.

First, let me say, I take full responsibility for my own actions and for those of my administration. As angry as I may be about activities undertaken without my knowledge, I am still accountable for those activities. As disappointed as I may be in some who served me, I'm still the one who must answer to the American people for this behavior. . . .

A few months ago I told the American people I did not trade arms for hostages. My heart and my best intentions still tell me that's true, but the facts and evidence tell me it is not. . . .

Much has been said about my management style. . . . The way I work is to identify the problem, find the right individuals to do the job, and then let them go to it. . . . When it came to managing the NSC staff, let's face it, my style didn't match its previous track record. I've already begun correcting this. . . .

By the time you reach my age, you've made plenty of mistakes. And if you've lived your life properly—you learn. You put things in perspective. You pull your energies together. You change. You go forward.

My fellow Americans, I have a great deal that I want to accomplish with you and for you over the next two years.

And the Lord willing, that's exactly what I intend to do. Good night, and God bless you.

It was a speech we all wished he never had to deliver. Even still, it was vintage Reagan. He took responsibility for the misconduct of his staff. He spoke plainly and candidly. And he did so in a way that made you know he was contrite. In today's post–September 11, 2001, world, where terrorist threats abound and American and other hostages are filmed being beheaded, perhaps the administration's actions may be viewed differently than they were back then. Indeed, no American would object to a president's resolve to save the life of one of our own.

But the thing about Reagan's speech was that he didn't cast blame, point fingers, or concoct conspiracy theories about how his enemies were out to get him. That wasn't the man's style. Instead, he stood in the gap, looked into the camera, and accepted responsibility for his actions and the misdeeds of others.

Reagan had weathered the storm. But he wasn't content to just fade into obscurity. He had things left to accomplish. The Revolution marched on. Indeed, bursting through the clouds were two shining achievements that would secure Ronald Reagan's place in history as "the last lion of the twentieth century," as Jack Kemp once called him.

The first of these occurred on June 12, 1987, in West Berlin, Germany at the Brandenburg Gate. I'll never forget meeting with the president in the Oval Office to review a draft of the speech he planned to deliver.

Anytime a president speaks on issues of national security, the State Department and others review his remarks. And one of the chief complaints from speechwriters, communications directors, and strategists is that the policy wonks end up ruining the spirit of the president's rhetoric by cutting out important statements.

Well, this speech proved no different. The debate centered on one particular passage of the president's speech, which had been largely crafted by a smart young wordsmith by the name of Peter Robinson. But as I discussed the issue with the president, it was clear he'd already chosen sides.

"I want it to stay in, Dick. It's what I want to say," he said.

"Mr. President, I agree with you. But you know the diplomats are going to give us trouble on this one," I said.

"Let them. I want it in," he replied.

When he took that steely tone with you, you always knew he had made up his mind. It reminded me of the way his voice sounded way back in 1980 when he had hurled the pages of his speech at me in his bedroom. But unlike that experience, this time his tone was music to my ears.

I was glad the line would stand. One of the many privileges of serving a president is that you often know what he will say before he says it. For example, in his speeches you know when the moments of rhetorical drama are about to crest. And as he inches closer and closer to those passages, your heartbeat quickens.

Here it comes, you think. *Just five more lines.*

Now four.

Three more to go.

Two.

One . . .

Then, as your eyes make a final pass across the faces of the audience, he releases, for all the entire world to hear, the words you hope will echo through time.

On June 12, 1987, that's exactly what happened.

Sticking to his rhetorical guns, Reagan fired words at a wall. And as he did, that wall began to shatter.

There is one sign the Soviets can make that would be unmistakable, that would advance dramatically the cause of freedom and peace.

General Secretary Gorbachev, if you seek peace, if you seek prosperity for the Soviet Union and Eastern Europe, if you seek liberalization: Come here to this gate! Mr. Gorbachev, open this gate! Mr. Gorbachev, tear down this wall!

I understand the fear of war and the pain of division that afflict this continent—and I pledge to you my country's efforts to help overcome these burdens. To be sure, we in the West must resist Soviet expansion. So we must maintain defenses of unassailable strength. Yet we seek peace; so we must strive to reduce arms on both sides.

Lady Margaret Thatcher, one of President Reagan's closest allies and a former client of mine, famously noted that Ronald Reagan won the cold war without firing a shot. But I have to tell you that even she sometimes had reservations about the force with which he spoke.

Once, when I was working on her campaign, she invited me to have dinner with her at No. 10 Downing Street. That evening she expressed some major reservations about what she viewed as the president's aggressive policies concerning the Soviets. She assumed he was overreaching and much too ambitious in his move to establish world peace. As I listened to her speak in her elegant cadence, I realized that even the "Iron Lady" wasn't so sure about the president's rhetorical approach in dealing with the Soviets. But as she and the rest of the world came to learn, his strategy had been right all along.

The reason was that Reagan understood that a president's words are *themselves* a form of action. Indeed, given the executive's limited constitutional powers, a president has essentially two options: words or weapons. But Reagan viewed the former as a form of the latter. By harnessing the indignation of Germans on both sides of the wall, Reagan's words became an army of jackhammers, pounding away at the evil edifice. Once the cries for liberation burst forth in response, it was all over.

The wall , and all it stood for, had been riven by a desire for the greatest longing of the human heart: freedom.

Six months after "Tear Down This Wall," Reagan would see another shining achievement. Even though Mr. Gorbachev had yet to tear down the wall, he was now willing to begin dismantling a portion of his nuclear arsenal. When the two men met in Geneva, both had agreed they would visit each other's countries. In December of 1987, the general secretary honored his pledge when he attended the Washington Summit to negotiate a possible Intermediate Nuclear Forces (INF) treaty. Gorbachev and Reagan signed the treaty, making it the first arms control agreement between the two superpowers to include the destruction of nuclear weapons.

More than that, though, INF was the culmination of Reagan's communication strategy vis-à-vis the Soviets, a rhetoric that strategically toggled between warmth and strength. All the way back in his days in Hollywood, he had warned against Marxist-Leninist expansion. Later, before a group of Christians in Orlando, Florida, he had declared the Soviet Union to be the focus of evil in the modern world. Then, at a summerhouse in Geneva overlooking a tranquil lake, he extended warm interpersonal dialogue. A year later this warmth turned cold when he gave a clenched-jaw response to an unacceptable offer in Iceland. And now his breathtaking challenge at the Brandenburg Gate had given way to a historic friendship between himself and the leader of an empire he once called evil. Yes, one could say Reagan's words *were* his weapons. Though thunderous in tone, they helped create a more peaceful world. And that, after all, had been his goal all along.

So much happened, so much was accomplished, over those eight years.

When Ronald Reagan entered the White House in 1980, America was suffocating under the weight of double-digit inflation; record-high interest rates had strangled economic growth; soaring tax burdens and regulations had choked innovation and investment; and American military muscle had atrophied from years of neglect.

But by the end of President Reagan's two terms, inflation had been tamed; the prime rate had been cut in half; his 1986 Tax Reform Act gave the United States the lowest federal individual and corporate income tax rates of any major industrialized nation in the world; personal tax rates were the lowest since the year 1931, saving the median-income American family almost $6,000 from what they would have paid under pre-1980 tax laws; 17.8 million new jobs had been created, over half of which went to women; African American employment was up 28 percent; the Carter "misery index" was chopped in half; and the United States and the Soviet Union had signed the first arms control agreement in history to reduce, as opposed to merely limit, the buildup of nuclear arms.

These historic achievements produced a somewhat ironic result. The very man who declared that government was the problem and not the solution ended up washing away much of the cynicism Americans harbored about the federal government's level of effectiveness in dealing with the crucial problems facing the country. Put another way, Reagan built confidence in government by communicating his lack of confidence in government.

In 1980, I asked Americans whether they agreed or disagreed with the following question: "As the government is now organized, it is hopelessly incapable of dealing with all the crucial problems facing the country today." Fifty-one percent agreed with this statement, while 45 percent disagreed. In 1988 I asked the same question. After eight years of Reagan's leadership, those numbers had undergone a net change of 19 percent, with only 42 percent agreeing and 55 disagreeing. The Reagan Revolution had swept away the malaise-filled years that preceded it.

Even more astounding was the near 180-degree turnaround in American attitudes about the prospects for the future, the president's favorite subject. In February of 1981, just one month after Reagan's inauguration, I asked Americans this question: "As we near the end of the year, which of the following do you think is likely to be true of the coming year? We will have a year filled with trouble, or we will have a year filled with peace?" At the beginning of Ronald Reagan's term, only 37 percent believed it would be a peaceful year, whereas 63 percent said it would be a year filled with trouble. By November 1988, those numbers had virtually flipped. Only 35 percent felt trouble was on the way, whereas 60 percent felt it would be a peaceful year.

Finally, American perceptions about how Ronald Reagan had done as president reveal that voters were paying attention. I calculated the president's approval margin—the difference between how many people approve versus how many disapprove—on several key issues. The results were amazing. For example, Reagan's approval margin on Soviet relations was 73 percent; on world peace it was 64 percent; on inspiring pride and confidence he enjoyed a 57 percent margin of approval; on arms control 46 percent; on unemployment he was at 22 percent; and on the economy 19 percent. Indeed, the only issue where the margin of disapproval was more than his approval margin was on governmental spending, where he was given a 29 percent margin of disapproval.

When asked about his most significant failures and successes, Americans had very definite impressions. Not surprisingly, 20 percent of voters felt that the president's most significant failure was the Iran-contra affair. The next most frequently cited failure (16 percent) was increased deficits. After that, all other responses were in low single digits.

As for President Reagan's most significant accomplishments, four responses topped the list. At 17 percent, his most commonly cited accomplishment was improved Soviet relations. His second and third most commonly cited achievements were reducing unemployment and improving the economy, both of which received 12 percent each. Ten percent of Americans said that Ronald Reagan's most significant accomplishment had been his historic arms agreements designed to create a more peaceful world.

Those final days of the second term were a time of sweetness and sorrow, but mostly sweetness. The boy from Dixon, Illinois, had come to Washington, D.C., with a vision and had turned it into a reality. Through words of strength and caring, Ronald Reagan had persuaded us to achieve great things by touching our most deeply held values. And for the final time as president of the United States, he would do so again in his farewell to the nation. On January 11, 1989, the Greatest Communicator looked up from his desk in the Oval Office and spoke:

> We've been together eight years now, and soon it'll be time for me to go. But before I do, I wanted to share some thoughts, some of which I've been saving for a long time.
>
> It's been the honor of my life to be your president. . . .
>
> One of the things about the presidency is that you're always somewhat apart. You spend a lot of time going by too fast in a car someone else is driving, and seeing the people through tinted glass— the parents holding up a child, and the wave you saw too late and couldn't return. And so many times I wanted to stop and reach out from behind the glass, and connect. Well, maybe I can do a little of that tonight. . . .
>
> The way I see it, there were two great triumphs, two things that I'm proudest of. One is the economic recovery, in which the people of America created—and filled— 19 million new jobs. The other is the recovery of our

morale. America is respected again in the world and looked to for leadership. . . .

And in all of that time I won a nickname, "The Great Communicator." But I never thought it was my style or the words I used that made a difference: It was the content. I wasn't a great communicator, but I communicated great things, and they didn't spring full bloom from my brow, they came from the heart of a great nation—from our experience, our wisdom, and our belief in principles that have guided us for two centuries. They called it the Reagan Revolution. Well, I'll accept that, but for me it always seemed more like the great rediscovery, a rediscovery of our values and our common sense. . . .

We've done our part. And as I walk off into the city streets, a final word to the men and women of the Reagan Revolution, the men and women across America who for eight years did the work that brought America back. My friends: We did it. We weren't just marking time. We made a difference. We made the city stronger. We made the city freer, and we left her in good hands. All in all, not bad, not bad at all.

There are men, few though they may be, who live their lives with the quiet confidence that comes from knowing how fleeting, how ephemeral, life truly is. They reject the frivolity of fame, awards, medals, and titles, and thus shy from the accolades most people spend their lives chasing. Wealth and power they find unimpressive—boring even.

No, what truly excites them, the things they can't ever seem to stop thinking about, are ideas and people.

They appreciate the simple things like laughter and time spent with family and stories told grandly. And you will know them by the way they walk, a facile stride filled with grace and a certain reassuring lack of self-awareness that gathers people up in its wake.

Ronald Reagan was one such man, and in 1968, I became one of the millions he swept up behind him.

Maybe you were one too.

That he gave us the privilege to benefit firsthand from his leadership is a debt none of us can ever repay. What we can do—what he'd want us to do—is to continue marching forward, armed with the strength and grace and humility he displayed throughout the Revolution. He dreamed, fought, persevered, and, above all else, had fun. And I believe he'd want us to do the same. Yes, I think he would want us to "win one for the Gipper."

Ronald Reagan transformed our lives and the lives of people around the world by embracing his "rendezvous with destiny."

And, in the end, what a destiny it was.

7

Three Goodbyes

But as long as we remember our first principles and believe in ourselves, the future will always be ours. . . . Once you begin a great movement, there's no telling where it will end. We meant to change a nation and, instead, we changed a world.

—Ronald Reagan, Farewell Address, January 11, 1989

The date was January 20, 1989.

George H. W. Bush had just been sworn in as the forty-first president of the United States. Outside the White House, the newly inaugurated president, Mrs. Bush, and the Quayles escorted Ronald and Nancy Reagan to a waiting helicopter. The Reagans ascended the steps to the aircraft, and the Gipper turned to face us all before snapping off a salute to the country he had served so well. Moments later, as they hovered just above their former home of eight years, now-citizen Ronald Reagan turned to Nancy, pointed out the window, and said, over the noise of whirling helicopter blades, "Look, dear, there's our little bungalow."

As the Reagans floated away into the Washington sky, they carried with them a lifetime of joys, hopes, fears, and memories. But for the fortieth president of the United States, the last of these would not endure. Indeed, in the years following his days as president, there would be three goodbyes, and my friend of thirty-six years would remember none of them. Each was at once painful and sweet. And, just as the Greatest Communicator would have wanted it, all three would remind me of the things that Ronald Reagan taught me about politics, leadership, and life.

The first goodbye would come from Ronald Reagan himself. It would be simple and graceful and courageous, and it would take the world's breath away. On November 5, 1994, Americans awoke to find in their newspapers a one-page letter that Reagan had written by himself.

> My Fellow Americans,
>
> I have recently been told that I am one of the millions of Americans who will be afflicted with Alzheimer's disease.
>
> Upon learning this news, Nancy and I had to decide whether as private citizens we would keep this a private matter or whether we would make this news known in a public way.
>
> In the past Nancy suffered from breast cancer and I had my cancer surgeries. We found through our open disclosures we were able to raise public awareness. We were happy that as a result many more people underwent testing.
>
> They were treated in early stages and able to return to normal, healthy lives.
>
> So now, we feel it is important to share it with you. In opening our hearts, we hope this might promote greater awareness of this condition. Perhaps it will encourage a clearer understanding of the individuals and families who are affected by it.
>
> At the moment I feel just fine. I intend to live the

remainder of the years God gives me on this earth doing the things I have always done. I will continue to share life's journey with my beloved Nancy and my family. I plan to enjoy the great outdoors and stay in touch with my friends and supporters.

Unfortunately, as Alzheimer's disease progresses, the family often bears a heavy burden. I only wish there was some way I could spare Nancy from this painful experience. When the time comes I am confident that with your help she will face it with faith and courage.

In closing let me thank you, the American people, for giving me the great honor of allowing me to serve as your President. When the Lord calls me home, whenever that may be, I will leave with the greatest love for this country of ours and eternal optimism for its future.

I now begin the journey that will lead me into the sunset of my life. I know that for America there will always be a bright dawn ahead.

Thank you, my friends. May God always bless you.
Sincerely,
Ronald Reagan

In 349 words, Ronald Reagan had reminded America of what made him the Greatest Communicator. He didn't fight against fate. He could have let the letter slip, dodging the most painful issue of his and Nancy's life together. But he didn't. Instead, armed with courage, dignity, and grace, he told the citizens whom he loved goodbye. He took his bow.

Knowing Nancy the way I was privileged to over those many years, I can only imagine the emptiness and fear she must have felt the first time she read it. To see his gentle plea for us to protect and comfort her when her "Ronnie" no longer could, well, it must have been devastating. Yet in the time between his leaving office and the drafting of his letter—the first of three goodbyes—the president and I shared many sweet moments, each reinforcing the things Ronald Reagan had taught me all those years.

On one occasion I visited him at his Los Angeles offices just after Valentine's Day. His mood that day was upbeat but tired. Fred Ryan, the president's assistant, had informed me that he had been up until midnight at a social with Zsa Zsa Gabor. One can only imagine what that must have been like.

The president greeted me warmly, just as he had always done. As we sat down I noticed two thick blue books on his desk. He scooped them up and held them out to me.

"Here, these are for you, Dick." With wide, giving eyes he said gently, "I thought you could use these. I want you to have them."

As I took the big volumes from his hands, I turned them on their sides to read the spines. When I saw what they were, I felt a lump form in my throat. They were compilations of Gallup polling data. At that time I had owned my international polling firm for twenty years. But, in his own sweet way, he thought his two books would be of use to me. It was the kind of a gift an ailing grandparent gives you, the type you'll never use but that you'll cherish for a lifetime. To this day, those volumes sit proudly on the shelves that line my office walls, and I wouldn't trade them for anything in this world.

Those books serve as a constant reminder of one of the most enduring lessons Ronald Reagan ever taught me. And that is this: *It's not all about us.*

For him, the most uncomfortable communicative moment was when he was the focus of attention. He always sought to tilt the conversational balance back in the other person's direction. Today, communication scholars have a fancy name for this; they call it "other-orientation." We just called it "being Ronald Reagan."

Go back and study his speeches. There you will find story after story, not of himself, but of ordinary people whom he thought extraordinary. Even in his letter to the nation, there is not one line, not a single word, that suggests self-pity. In fact, the only person he seems preoccupied with is his beloved Nancy. If any thought had the power to dent his optimism for the future it was that of Nancy having to walk through life alone.

Thinking of others was always his way. I remember once during the second term entering the Oval Office depressed and gloomy. I had bad news to report and dreaded doing so. Ever attuned to people's feelings, Reagan immediately picked up on my mood. After I walked him through some pretty somber findings, he interrupted by recalling the method by which he had achieved his highest ratings ever.

Smiling, he said, "Dick, don't worry about it. We'll be fine. Tell you what, I know what I'll do. I guess I'll just have to go out and get shot again."

One of the messages I believe Ronald Reagan would wish to send those who would lead our country in the future is to take time for people. In our increasingly aggressive and vitriolic political climate, I think the Greatest Communicator would say: *Slow down. Look around you. Don't see crowds, see faces.*

As I've shared throughout this book, doing the small, private acts of goodness was one of the things he loved most about being president. Children would color him a picture or write him a letter in their simple scrawl. And Reagan, the most powerful man on the planet, would take time out of his day to sit down and, in his own handwriting, respond to the things they had written. The reason the country is only now learning about his prolific correspondence is that he didn't want to cheapen his quiet acts of kindness by turning his letters into publicity stunts. Honestly, I always felt he got just as much pleasure, if not more, out of sending those letters as those who received them.

Yet his goodbye to the nation provided him with no joy. The moment I read it I knew I needed to pay him a visit. Still, somehow I couldn't quite wrap my mind around the seriousness of his condition. My optimism clouded my judgment. I figured there would still be significant time before the ravages of Alzheimer's disease began robbing him of the memories the old gang had shared over all those years. But there were two additional things that prevented me from accepting reality.

The first revolved around the fact that Valentine's Day had just passed. I told him that while buying my wife a Valentine's card I had been reminded of the time he asked me to purchase Nancy's anniversary card at Dulles International Airport. He laughed at the recollection.

"Well, Dick, I ended up giving Nancy her Valentine's card a day early. Sometimes I get the dates a little mixed up, you know. Nancy and I always exchange our valentines in bed when we wake up. I guess I got a little excited about giving her mine this year. The people up on the ranch found a tree that had rotted on one side. When they cut it down they found that the trunk made a perfect heart. So they cut me a three-inch slice out of this naturally formed heart. And I had them put my and Nancy's brand on it so I could give her a California three-inch oak valentine! I gave it to her and she chuckled and reminded me I was just a day early. I guess I got a little excited."

He'd had trouble remembering the date, but I didn't think anything of it. When you consider that presidents have every single minute of every day mapped out by staff, adjusting to keeping up with the details of everyday living could take some getting used to.

The second reason for my denial was that just a few months before his letter to the nation, he had given me the best gift one could ever receive from the Greatest Communicator—a speech that paid tribute to our friendship. My firm was celebrating its twenty-fifth anniversary, and a friend had, without my knowledge, invited the president to videotape a speech to be played at the event about our days together. The whole thing was a surprise. Along with the polling books, it remains one of my most treasured gifts from him.

But the problem was, I had seen him on film looking great for a man his age. What is so amazing about that speech is how you can still see flashes of all the Greatest Communicator's old instincts. His cadence was slower, but the tilt of the head, the "aw, shucks" shrug of the shoulder, the quick glance off camera when hitting his punch line, they were all still there. And these images allowed me to not accept things as they were, but rather as I wished them to be. I had taken solace in seeing all his rhetorical skills still present. However, little did I know how bad off he truly was at the time he delivered his tribute to me. I learned that his performance had been a true labor of love, another example of his selfless spirit. Indeed, many years later a member of his staff explained to me that his speech on my behalf was the last taped address he ever delivered. And although I didn't realize it at the time, my next visit to see Ronald Reagan would be my last.

The second goodbye came not too long after the first. Looking back on it all now, my first clue things were worse than they appeared should have been the difficulty I had setting up a meeting through his staff. Never in all my years with him had I experienced resistance to my seeing or calling the president. But this time was different. I don't fault his staff. They were doing what loyal friends should do—protecting his dignity and privacy. Finally, a meeting was set up.

When I walked into his office everything seemed fine. He was sitting at his desk just like always. When he realized someone had walked in the room, he looked up, cocked his head, and shot me that Irish grin I knew so well. As he stood to greet me, I extended my hand. *See there,* I thought, *same old Reagan I've always known and loved.*

Outwardly, he looked fine. Like his convictions, his hairstyle had never changed. The grip of his hand was still firm and steady. And that grin—well, it was there, too.

Nothing to worry about, I thought.

But that thought ended as quickly as it began.

"Well hello, Mr. President. It's so good to see you," I said.

"Well, thank you. Good to see you," he said.

But as our eyes met, I saw something I had never seen before. It was as if his mind was riffling through a mental Rolodex of the millions of faces he'd encountered over his life. From crowds, to speeches, to rope lines, to meetings, to parties . . . and not one of them matched mine.

He didn't know who I was; I was a stranger.

We sat down and had the most painful conversation I have ever had with anyone in my life. Gone was the fluidity of thought and speech. He was uncomfortable. And so was I. He would begin to say something, only to drift off into silence. I felt as though my presence was torture to his spirit.

As my eyes scanned the many pictures and books in his office, memories of political battles won and lost ricocheted through my mind. Images of old friends, paintings I'd seen before, books I knew he liked—they were all there. But these had all lost their meaning. They were now merely the wallpaper of his world.

I pointed to something on his shelf and said how much I liked it. For a brief second his eyes widened, and he got up from his chair and began walking across the room. I met him at his bookcase. He then did something I realized had become his routine. He took me from item to item, relic to relic, and said something about each one. He was trying to run out the clock on our discomfort. He said simple things, things like, "And here is a picture I really like," or, "Someone gave this to me." And with each item he handed me, I could feel the weight of his confusion grow.

Since 1968, I had looked forward to every minute shared with this man. But in that office, all I could think about was letting him get back to the tranquil serenity of the world in which he now lived.

Finally, our time was up. As I clasped his hand for the very last time, I felt my eyes begin to fill, and it was all I could do not to let the tears fall in his presence.

He had given me so much. I wanted him to know how grateful I was to have been granted the chance to learn from him all those years. I wanted to thank him for blessing me and my family with a life we never dreamed of. I wanted to tell him that no matter what, he would forever be my hero and friend. There was so much I wanted to say. But I wasn't the Greatest Communicator, he was.

The most powerful thing he did during our last meeting came not from what he said, but from what he left unsaid.

He never said "goodbye."

Even though, in essence, it was the second goodbye, to this day his omission is something that gives me great hope and, yes, even joy.

When I think about that final visit, I am reminded of Ronald Reagan's unique view of leadership. He saw his political career as a great current gathering off a distant shore. The presidency had been a glorious cresting wave, surging with momentum and energy. But then, once it had crashed and his legacy had cast its treasures upon America's shore, it was time for it to fade from view, return to the source from whence it came, and be absorbed back into the tides of history in order to lend its power to the wave to follow.

Future presidents must remember what Ronald Reagan never forgot: the presidency belongs to no one. It belongs to the people. It is an institution far greater than one human being. And that's why Ronald Reagan never took his coat off in the Oval Office—he wasn't in "his" office. He was a visitor, a temporary steward, and he never let himself or the power he possessed delude him into thinking otherwise.

If he were still with us, I believe he would encourage future presidential candidates to never forget that the political and economic power of America flows from a single current, and that is a citizenry that possesses an unrelenting, unyielding passion for one principle: freedom. The force thrusting Reagan's wave forward was the same force that will propel future presidents, and that is a citizenry that longs to keep America free and safe. The reason Ronald Reagan was interested in the mountains of data I collected on his behalf was not so he could engage in "finger to the wind" leadership. Rather, in a country of hundreds of millions, it was his way of *listening* to his boss, the American people.

Ronald Reagan led in a different time filled with different challenges. As we continue to come to grips with the generation-long war we must wage against terrorism, we realize that, in some ways, the tasks we face are even greater than those he dealt with. But as President George W. Bush so eloquently reminded a fearful nation in the days after September 11, 2001, while there is much that has changed, much has remained unchanged. As Bush said, "Freedom and fear, justice and cruelty, have *always* [emphasis mine] been at war, and we know that God is not neutral between them."

I think Ronald Reagan would want those words to be passed like a torch from one president to the next. The American story remains one of permanence and change. What Ronald Reagan taught me is this: *Presidents must listen, lead, and then leave.* When his time was up, Reagan relinquished power with dignity and grace. During our final visit, I realized the tragic beauty of his condition. His mind had followed the form of his philosophy of leadership: listen, lead, and then leave.

On June 5, 2004, like the *Challenger* astronauts he once eulogized so movingly, the president began his journey to another place.

It was a sad day when I learned my friend had died. Even though most of us who had been at his side all those years had already said our second goodbye, his passing and the memorial and funeral services that followed produced a third and final chance to recognize the man who helped America believe in itself again.

The national week of remembrance began with the president's body resting at the Reagan Library in Simi Valley, California, where he would eventually return after lying in state in the Capitol Rotunda.

The funeral services were almost worthy of the man, with all the symbols and signs of the passing of a great national soul— the twenty-one-gun salute, flags throughout the nation lowered to half-mast, the horse-drawn caisson, the reversed boots in the stirrups, and the entrance of the casket into the National Cathedral.

Entering from the rear of the cathedral, I sat on the right side of the sanctuary. My wife, Jeralie, and my eldest son, Rich, sat quietly in preparation for the service. Every face was a memory. There, a few rows away, sat the president's perennial thorn in the side, reporter Sam Donaldson. What times we had with Sam and his aggressive questions! And over there, in the distance, were Bill Clark and Ed Meese, two of the most devoted and long-term Reagan supporters. Later, I saw the president's smart and loyal secretary of labor, Ann McLaughlin. My friend Phil Dusenberry, the mastermind behind the beautifully crafted "Morning in America" ads, was there also. As was one of the most politically astute academics I've ever known, Marty Anderson, who was the driving force behind so many of President Reagan's domestic policies.

Then there were the world leaders. It had been a while since I had last seen Lady Margaret Thatcher. I had always been proud of my association with her through the years, but never more so than while listening to her tribute to the president. Despite her failing health, one could have hardly wished for a more stirring, eloquent rhetorical performance. In her rich, stately cadence she said of her friend "Ronnie":

For the final years of his life, Ronnie's mind was clouded by illness. That cloud has now lifted. He is himself again— more himself than at any time on this earth. For we may be sure that the Big Fella Upstairs never forgets those who remember Him.

And as the last journey of this faithful pilgrim took him beyond the sunset, and as heaven's morning broke, I like to think—in the words of Bunyan—that "all the trumpets sounded on the other side." We here still move in twilight. But we have one beacon to guide us that Ronald Reagan never had. We have his example. Let us give thanks today for a life that achieved so much for all of God's children.

Something tells me that Ronald Reagan got a kick out of hearing Lady Margaret Thatcher pronounce "Big Fella Upstairs" in her regal British accent.

I was touched by former President George H. W. Bush's short and tender speech. One of the things I wish more Americans knew about the former president is what a sensitive and sentimental man he truly is. He spoke as someone who had loyally and faithfully served his president and country. His dignity and class are hard to match, and in the simple elegance of his words and the feelings behind them, Ronald Reagan's former vice president served him well—yet again.

And of course, who could forget President George W. Bush's eulogy to the man he calls his political hero. The media were quick to draw comparisons between President Bush and Ronald Reagan, and I have often remarked that there are several parallels between the two men and their vision for an America that achieves peace through strength. Just as Ronald Reagan's "strident" rhetoric against the former Soviet Union was criticized, so too has Bush's oratory on the war on terror. But in this, Bush should take great comfort. History always has a way of vindicating those on the side of freedom.

As President Bush closed his speech, I felt he captured the essence of the man who defined my politics when he said of President Reagan:

And where does that strength come from? Where is that courage learned? It is the faith of a boy who read the Bible with his mom. It is the faith of a man lying in an operating room, who prayed for the one who shot him before he prayed for himself. It is the faith of a man with a fearful illness, who waited on the Lord to call him home.

Now death has done all that death can do. And as Ronald Wilson Reagan goes his way, we are left with the joyful hope he shared. In his last years, he saw through a glass darkly.

Now he sees his Savior face-to-face.

And we look to that fine day when we will see him again, all weariness gone, clear of mind, strong and sure, and smiling again, and the sorrow of his parting gone forever.

May God bless Ronald Reagan, and the country he loved.

As the service drew to a close, the cathedral echoed with the most majestic music imaginable. With somber, throbbing tones undulating through the air, Ronald Reagan's casket passed us all. Each person, in his or her own way, paid tribute to the president. Some lifted their hands to cross themselves. Others bowed in solemn prayer. And still others wiped tears from their eyes.

I was not among the latter, however. My tears had fallen several years before. Now, in that moment, sitting in that grand structure, I was filled with a quiet joy, a silent peace that my friend's pain was no more; that he was in a better place, just as President Bush had said. Ronald Reagan had always maintained that America's best days lay ahead. But in saying this, I suspect he also knew it to be true for himself, as well.

And then my heart turned toward Nancy. Never was there a more devoted, loving, protective spouse. She had willingly and joyfully built her world around him. But now she looked so frail, so weak, like her eyes couldn't cry any more. And I just prayed that she would find comfort and peace beyond the pain.

We all filtered out of the National Cathedral only to be greeted by an overcast Washington sky that mirrored our collective mood. Then one of the largest-ever gatherings of Reaganauts quickly ensued. We were all much grayer and slower and more weathered than we had been during the days when the Revolution was in full swing, but we were together again. And what a diverse lot we were. Yet despite all the differences, the terse words, and the personal battles, through it all there was love. Love of his principles, love of his values, love of the lessons he taught us, love of the man himself. Politics is a rough game, but moments like that reconfirm my belief that it remains a noble endeavor.

As I visited with the great Reagan band of brothers and sisters, it occurred to me that if someone were to ask each one present a version of the question President Reagan posed to Walter Mondale, namely: "Are you better off now because you knew Ronald Reagan up close and personal?" I am certain there would have been a resounding "Yes!" And I think he would have liked that.

The president's body was then transported back west, to the place where his political odyssey began. It was there that America witnessed what I believe would have surely been Ronald Reagan's most favored scene.

As the cavalcade of black Cadillacs made their way along the California highway leading to the president's westward-facing burial site, something amazing, something unexpected happened. Hundreds of thousands of everyday Americans, rich and poor, young and old, began lining the highways. People, thousands of them, pulled their cars off the road and into the emergency lanes. The overpasses looking down on the route the president's hearse was to take were thick with citizens who wanted to pay tribute to the man they loved. One man stood in the back of his pickup truck, tall and rigid, with his hand straight and taut, waiting for the chance to salute his commander in chief for the last time. Two fire engines had extended their ladders heavenward, at the top of which two firefighters bridged the gap between them with an American flag. The president's hearse drove underneath the man-made arch.

And speaking of flags, they were everywhere, something I know he would have loved. Ronald Reagan wore his patriotism on his sleeve. He never apologized for his pride in America, and he couldn't understand those who did.

As the caravan wound through the California hills, it left in its wake a streak of cheers, tears, and waving flags. It was California's way of welcoming home their favored son, of letting him know how deeply they felt about him, and that they would never forget the love and leadership he had shown.

The day would end with the Reagan children, Michael, Patty, and Ron, honoring their father in his native tongue—oratory. Each spoke about him in their own unique way, and in the process we realized what some had doubted. We realized that Ronald Reagan's children *knew* they were loved.

About public communication, the president used to say, "Dick, you've got to have a good opener and a good closer." Well, the president's closer would come as the sun dropped heavy in the California sky. The casket was set in its final resting place. This would, of course, be one of the most painful scenes to watch, as Nancy faced the reality of letting go of Ronnie.

She didn't want to.

None of us did.

But when it happened, as it had to, she spread herself over the top of the casket, as if to hug him one final time, before the children came to her side.

It was hard to watch.

And there was another scene that was hard to watch that day. One we must never forget. It involved some venomous attacks that were hurled by persons of narrow political persuasions. It is unfathomable to think that there are people to whom politics transcends all else. And yet this is what Ronald Reagan fought against all his political life. The word "fought" is critical, because revolutions do not occur by any other means. Reagan believed in fighting hard. He believed in standing firm. But he also believed it was important to disagree without being disagreeable. His epic friendship with Democratic Speaker of the House Tip O'Neill was a prime example of two politicians who could slug it out when the sun was up and be the dearest of friends when the sun went down. Today, all too often, we see a "shoot first and ask questions later" mentality. But what Ronald Reagan understood is that circumstances and people can change.

Take, for example, Mikhail Gorbachev and the former Soviet Union. One of the most powerful marks of the success of President Reagan was reflected not in the symbols of national honor but in the words of the former Russian general secretary when he said, "I shall always remember the years working together with President Reagan, putting an end to confrontation between our two countries, and equally, our friendly rapport, which revealed Ronald's human qualities." So, people change. And while politics was one of Reagan's passions, it was not his greatest passion. This he reserved for people.

This was the core of what he taught me. He taught me to care about people, to hold fast to worthy and worthwhile goals, to love more the United States of America, and to cherish and fight for freedom.

In short, Ronald Reagan taught me to be a better American, and his unique reference to what our destiny would be—a shining city on a hill—illuminated not only the lives of those who worked alongside him, but also those of the tens of millions of people who are better off today because of his leadership.

Ronald Reagan will remain one of the greatest communicators because his words transcend time. He joins that select group of orators whose words have reshaped the contours of history toward noble ends. The greatest statesman and orator Rome ever produced, Marcus Tullius Cicero, once wrote, "But the man who equips himself with the weapons of eloquence, not to be able to attack the welfare of his country but to defend it, he, I think, will be a citizen most helpful and most devoted both to his own interests and those of his community."

In the end, that was Ronald Wilson Reagan: a man who used words to make the world a better place.

Epilogue

There is a final thing I feel I must say.

If there is any barrier, any obstacle between us and our understanding of Ronald Reagan, it exists in the zeitgeist of our age, not in the man himself. In a culture of postmodern indifference, where cynicism is obligatory and little else sacred, Reagan remains for some an alien and stranger in a foreign land. His optimism, his principles, his faith—these seem so far away, so remote. Yet these limitations of imagination belong to us, not him.

This business about the "mysteriousness" of Reagan is itself a mystery to me. *Every* life lived well possesses a degree of mystery, a word unspoken, a thought unshared. And in this, Reagan was no different. But beyond that, beyond the normal degree of opacity we all possess, Ronald Reagan lived perhaps the most transparent life of any modern American president.

Reagan's secret was that he didn't have any secrets.

The thing that baffles so many of the doubters is how a person could be so optimistic, so full of hope, so caring, yet not be pretending. He was not perfect. He had flaws. But there was always a "too good to be true" quality about the man. And in his death, I suspect this will only grow.

For the doubters, Reagan's Hollywood roots made them wary of his methods and motives; they believed the image they had seen in the media of an unyielding, fiery, conservative demagogue.

But as any great actor will attest, the best actors don't act, they *become*.

And that is the way I'll always remember the man I served all those years, as one who *became* something for everyone.

He became a storyteller.

He became a comforter.

He became a protector.

He became a comedian.

He became a friend.

Above all else, he became what we needed him to because he believed it was his destiny to reignite the American economy, lift the Damocles sword of nuclear annihilation, and make us believe in ourselves again.

A final story.

Once, Reagan and I were visiting in the Oval Office when he brought up the parable of the Good Samaritan. He said, "You know, it is often overlooked that the person who *really* gained the most was the Good Samaritan who rendered service, not the person who received it. I think the real lesson of the parable is that we benefit most when we help a neighbor in need."

There is perhaps no better summary of Ronald Reagan's view of his presidency and life. In his mind, America didn't owe him thanks. He owed America thanks for giving him the chance to serve. That may sound simple, but it's true.

Like the others, I was there. We saw him on planes, buses, trains, cars, stages, in hotels, homes, the Oval Office, at dinner, on the phone, meeting with friends, meeting with citizens . . . and I'll have you know, he was always the same person.

He was, as he will always be, the Greatest Communicator.